100k

ANDRE RAY

100k
Copyright © 2016 by Andre Ray
ALL RIGHTS RESERVED

ISBN-13: 978-1532945502

ISBN-10: 1532945507

Editor: Stacey Debono / sdebonoediting@gmail.com
Cover Design: Stacey Debono

Social Media:
Twitter - https://twitter.com/dtbvisions
Instagram - https://www.instagram.com/dtbvisions/
Email - creativedre@gmail.com

This book is dedicated to my grandparents, Thomas J. Swisher and Mary Swisher, who I often referred to as Daddy and Mama.

ACKNOWLEDGEMENTS

First and foremost I thank God;. without Him I wouldn't be here. There were so many circumstances and situations in my life that overcame me and there just seemed to be no way out, but God guided me through the fire. Thank you in the name of Jesus Christ Almighty, there is power in His name.

My wife Natoya, she never counted me out when so many did. My Toy stayed by my side, giving me the best she has to offer: love. I love you always! Thanks, babe.

My kids Nyiesha, Mary, Tobias, and Andreya. I strive to be a better man and person for you guys, and I love each of you deeply.

Thomas J. Swisher, my grandfather, who taught me how to be a man in more ways than one. His insight and outlook on life helped me through many storms. Without my grandfather (whom I often called Daddy) I wouldn't be half the man I am today. I am forever grateful to my daddy.

To all of my friends and family who encouraged me to write this book, thank you.

The power of visualization:
you have to see yourself in the
position that you want.

TABLE OF CONTENTS

FOREWORD

Written by Natoya Ray

I am a living witness to what Andre is talking about in this book. His desire and ability to see his goals and make them a reality is amazing. His desire comes from counting hundreds of thousands of dollars back in the day. I sometimes laugh to myself when I think about how he was chasing this money like a crack head chases that first hit. He has made everyone in our household a hustler. His ability to make his goals a reality comes from God making him humble, loyal, and is a great example to his family and friends. He has always been a goal-oriented person.

I clearly remember the night of 12/25/96, the height of Andre's bad boy days, the day that his life changed forever. We were driving up the hill on our way to his house, and back then Andre loved listening to Tupac, so of course one of his songs was playing in the CD deck. When we reached his house, something wasn't right. Flashing lights and DEA agents wearing their signature blue jackets with the yellow block letters were everywhere; Andre knew that his life as a drug dealer had ended.

We were both arrested; I was released but Andre's problems were just beginning. He was charged with possession of a controlled substance (cocaine) with the intent to sell, and possession of more than ten kilograms of powder cocaine, which enhanced the charges. This was a dark time in his life. I'm not going to go into any details about that time in his life because that is for him to talk about, but I will say that despite his ordeals, his ability to make something out of himself after all of that is fascinating. Most people go back to the streets and repeat the cycle, but not Andre. He was determined to make something positive out of his life.

I remember a dream Andre had after coming home from being incarcerated. He explained to me that in his dream he was walking and he came to a fork in the road. To the left he saw burning debris and acres of land in total flames and ruin. He could feel the heat from the flames on the left side of his body. In the midst of the flames was a sign that listed all things unholy or displeasing to God; things such as premarital sex, adultery, lying, cheating, murder, etc. Most dreams do not make any sense, like this sign burning in the field, but it was still legible. This took on a significant meaning to Andre. He then turned to the right and the land was prosperous and fertile, the total opposite of the left side. A sign on the right side listed all of the good things such as happiness, love, peace, and prosperity.

Andre woke up with the dream fresh on his mind and perceived the dream as a warning. It was clear that the left side represented the wages of sin and death, and the right side was life. He saw it as a sign of choices that we all make in life, and the road to the left led to certain death. If he chose to travel down the road to the right, Andre would be on a road that lead to joy, peace, and a sense of fulfillment. He chose the road to the right, the road to a better life. There is a heavenly reward for worshiping God and traveling the right path in life; this is how Andre interpreted his dream. I personally think his dream was the Holy Spirit guiding him to the right path.

Andre had a plan. He went to barber college and learned his trade. Andre has a gift of drawing and I truly believe he cuts hair so well because his job is tied into this talent he has been blessed with. This is how he enhances all of his clients' features as it relates to a haircut.

Andre completed barber college, took the state exam and passed on his first attempt. This was a huge accomplishment for him because a large number of barber grads fail the first time.

He found a building for his business on 89th Avenue in Oakland, California; we cleaned it up and laid the floor down. I actually helped to lay the floor down! That was the first time he or I have ever installed a floor together. Cleaning up a space and even painting interior walls is fairly simple, but to actually get on my hands and knees to complete the floor from one end to another was big for me. We did it together, and he and I were both impressed. He bought chairs, stations, mirrors, and Creative Reflections Barber Shop was launched. One of his goals was made into a reality; he had his own business!

He kept a 'goal board' in his barber shop against the wall in front of his cutting station, and on this board were all of his goals for the next five years. It was disguised to the public; there were business cards placed all over the board and only Andre saw and understood his goals on that board. He read his goals several times a day and visualized them happening. Not only visualizing but imagining the feeling that accomplishing those goals would bring. Hard work and dedication, working long nights and early mornings cutting hair and making his own line of t-shirts (Ridaz Wear) allowed him to turn those goals into reality.

Ridaz Wear was a t-shirt line that he started in order to earn more cash. Andre knew the only way to really have more earning potential was to cut out the middle man and print his own product. He purchased a silk screen machine and all of the equipment that was needed to start printing. He knew nothing about printing an image onto a shirt whatsoever, but that didn't stop him. He basically taught himself through trial and error and asked people questions who were knowledgeable in the field. This was the pre-YouTube era...amazing.

Andre wanted to strengthen his credit score because part of his plans was to buy a home. He started building his credit by paying off old debts and got a loan for a car - an Impala SS that he had been wanting for some time but refused to buy because the timing wasn't right. Andre has a saying: "Sacrifice today for a better tomorrow", which means put off today the things that you want and take care of your needs today. Focus on your needs, not the wants. The wants in life will keep you broke. Save as much money as you can for the best opportunities. If there isn't a need, nine times out of ten you shouldn't purchase it.

The car was a piece of the puzzle to the bigger picture. By him paying off debt and opening up a line of credit and financing the car were moves that helped bring that picture into focus. A home was the bigger picture. In 2000 he bought our first home at 1223 77th Avenue in Oakland; Andre said we would live there for five years and then buy another house. His goals consisted of purchasing more properties from which he could draw income. Every year he wanted to purchase income property.

In 2001 the U.S. Marshall arrested Andre for the same case that he had fought back in 1996. Even though it had been dismissed twice, the United States Supreme Court ruled against him. A warrant was issued and served. He fought it but eventually pleaded out and received five years in the penitentiary. This was a difficult dilemma and put all of his plans and goals on hold. He ended up doing almost three years of that five year sentence.

When Andre began doing his time, real estate prices were rising. He knew that the market was going to change for the better which is why he planned on purchasing every year. His prison term affected us, his family, greatly. We went from a unit united by love and

4

respect for each other to feeling separated and lonely.

Andre paroled in 2004 and immediately planned his life for the next year. His plan was to work hard at becoming one of the best barbers in Oakland and also to buy me a Yukon truck, free and clear with no monthly car note. He said, "Give me one year. I'll have the shop cranking hard, then I will refinance our home for a lower interest rate and pull some money out and buy you a new truck." The year passed quickly, and true to his word I got my truck - a 2006 GMC Yukon, paid for completely with all cash. The shop was doing very well.

The following year, he bought 1338 99th Avenue in Oakland. We still owned the previous property as well. Originally the idea was to fix it up and rent it out, but we quickly changed our minds and decided to sell it.

The property sold for $460,000, not bad at all. The home on 77th was purchased for $80,000 and a little over five years later we sold it for $460,000. We refinanced the loan on the home in order to secure a lower interest rate and to pull out some cash - $160,000. Add that to the original mortgage $160,000 + $80,000 = $240,000, which was the new mortgage. Our mortgage went from roughly $800 a month to almost $1,400 a month. One year later we sold the house for $460,000. That's $220,000 profit plus the $160,000 that was cashed out the year before, all in a five year time frame. What job has that type of earning power in such a short amount of time?

In 2011, we built a home from the ground up. Between 2006 and 2011 he also bought two other properties. One has two homes on it – we rent them out which also creates extra income. This is testament to the power of will and desire to be more than what you see every day and what people think of you. Andre has told me that people always think the worst because of a person's past or by the way that person looks. He believed in himself and accomplished his goal, and continues to do this. *You* can do it too.

This book is a real gift to you if you want to build your credit, if you want to start your own business, or if you want to buy a house. Hard work and persistence is the key. Believe in yourself; whatever you desire to have and build, you can do it. You cannot get distracted by what others are doing, saying, or by the set backs in life. You have to have excellent credit to get the best rates, and work hard and save your money to get ahead in life. Your past does not predict your future. Everything in this book is a testament to a true story – it takes a hell of a man to want to share this information to help others better their lives.

Andre has lived in the fast lane - money, cars, guns, and females; those days are over now. He is now dedicated to helping those that are in that life which will inevitably lead to death or jail. Use what you have to motivate yourself and turn it into a life long investment for your future. If you are not in the fast lane and may just not believe in yourself, if you have just given up because everything seems bad, or if you just need guidance, this informational and proven-to-work book can help you get on the right track and inspire you to make your dreams come true.

CHAPTER 1
(HIS)TORY

This is a testament of the power of the human mind. You see, if properly nourished, all things can become a reality. If you feed the mind wholesome thoughts and follow them through, you will grow strong, living a life worth living. Feed the mind junk and your demise will follow. Demise, not only in physical death, but also in the sense of poverty, jealousy, unhappiness, etc.

In this book, you will find an 'escape plan'; these pages can and will help you, if applied correctly, to escape a life of poverty. Bold words I know, but true. How far away from the depths of poverty is totally up to you. Someone might read this and think, "This is not for me", but the person who reads and applies these principles will surely get ahead in life. I'm not proclaiming that you will become rich, although the possibility is most definitely there. This book will take you to a level above or more in your financial status right now, and will open your mind to other possibilities that can take you to even more levels.

I do not claim to be an expert or some type of guru, but I know the things that are disclosed within these pages from experience. If there is something in these pages that I have not personally experienced, I have researched it thoroughly and found it to be the truth. I will show you how to save and invest that money you have saved. You should pay yourself first all the time. And why not? You've been paying everyone else first all of your life, now is the time to pay you. You deserve it. Stop being a consumer and be an investor *in yourself.* A few simple methods can change your life, methods I've employed throughout my life. Some are fairly easy, while others may take a little self-discipline.

Take control of your finances and you will be able to control your destiny, otherwise you risk living a life unfulfilled. You must prepare for the future or you will always be in need. How can you expect to eat a great meal if you haven't prepared it? In order to live a life where money and lack of it isn't part of the equation, a certain amount of preparation will be required.

If you have ever thought to yourself, "I want to change my life. There has to be a better way!" then take control and make your life worth living. Take vacations, buy that car you want, and just get out there and experience life. However, if you are not prepared financially it can be catastrophic and/or impossible. I do not recommend that anyone spend any amount of money just to make themselves feel better. Most people are just taking it as it comes, living paycheck to paycheck, going with the flow. I've been there; going with the flow will get you exactly what the majority of people have now, *nothing.*

I remember one year I was really feeling

bummed out because I had just paid my taxes. Man, taxes can be a real burden when you owe the IRS. I was hungry and decided on a burger and fries. As I was waiting on my food, Mike, a friend of mine, drove into the parking lot.

Mike ordered his food and sat at my table. Idle chit chat back and forth, you know, how you been, how is the family? Then Mike started talking about his car and how every year he would buy another brand new car then sell the old one to his sister for $1. He went on to say that he owned 24 properties, and I was stunned. Pretty amazing for a guy that drove public transportation for a living. I never knew that he had accomplished a feat of this magnitude. I've never known anyone who owned more than one home, and usually it was the grandparents who owned it. Home ownership was rare in the black community. When I was growing up in Oakland, California, I saw that most families were single parent households living on government assistance, welfare, or Section 8. But Mike owned 24 properties. That is huge for anyone.

Mike was living a life most people from my neck of the woods could only dream of. He had my full attention; he had came from humble beginnings and was from the neighborhood, drove public transportation, and made a modest living...or so I thought.

He asked me if I wanted to have the ability to buy a new car every year, or to one day be financially secure. "Of course, who wouldn't?" was my response. Mike explained to me the importance of home ownership then offered to take me on a tour of some of his properties. I had nothing planned for the day so off we went. He also put me in contact with his real estate broker. That was huge for me, I really needed to hear and see it all.

Too often someone will know a better way but will not reveal it. If that person is doing well, they won't talk about it. We need more success stories so that people can see and believe that they too can make it out of bad situations financially. My grandma used to say to me, "If you don't have any money, then you're going to do something in order to get it." She was right. Some people turn to crime because of a sense of hopelessness. Crime for most becomes a way out but in reality it's a dead end, figuratively and literally.

Mike was a millionaire on the low. At that time of my life I hadn't met anyone who had amassed such financial wealth legally. The majority of people I came in contact with were hard working individuals or drug dealers that never seemed to get ahead in life. Working class people were clocking in and out just to live paycheck to paycheck. The drug dealer, well, that lifestyle is obvious; it seems to be good at first but then one of two things will happen: jail or death. Even knowing that you don't stand a chance, kids in the hood will still try their luck even though the odds are against them.

Talking to someone I knew that was in fact a millionaire showed me that it *can* be done. I always thought of millionaires as flashy and flamboyant. You know, like the type you might see on TV. Mike proved not to be that stereotypical millionaire. After spending some time with him, I made up my mind that I was going to advance myself and have a positive attitude. A positive attitude is more appealing than a negative one and will determine how far you go in life.

***

I come from the city of dope / Can't be saved by John the Pope, lyrics from the Too Short song, "City of Dope" from his *Life is Too Short* album. Too Short spit the harsh and gritty lyrics of my hometown, Oakland. Growing up in Oakland was challenging because of the environment. Most of my friends came from a single parent household and that parent almost always was the mom, who was usually addicted to drugs. Now I'm not saying that all households were broken and that all moms were addicted to drugs in Oakland, but unfortunately most of my friends and kids I came in contact with came from these environments.

I was fortunate that my grandparents raised me which provided me with a stable, two parent household. There was always someone home so the sense of family and structure was there. For most of my friends and associates, this environment was non-existent. Even with a strong family support system, my outside environment held more weight partly because of money issues; I'd also seen my peers sell dope as if it was legal without any recourse whatsoever. It was only a matter of time before I jumped in with both feet.

I was one of those guys that felt a sense of hopelessness and desperation. I had to do something to change my reality and the only thing I knew was what I saw most of my peers doing - selling dope. It seemed to be working for them at the time. The people I knew that were slangin' dope had fancy cars and dressed well. I wanted in.

Crack was the drug of choice throughout the '80s and '90s. It was a thriving underworld business that didn't require a degree or experience; a desire to earn money was the only qualification.

I always had a huge desire to have big money. Every kid in the inner city wishes to change their reality and I wasn't any different. I was raised by my grand-parents who basically couldn't afford another mouth to feed, but they did their best to raise me right and to supply the basics - shelter, food, and clothing.

I decided to earn money on my own, so I started selling crack in my neighborhood. My hood was known as Dag Vill. It's a small neighborhood in comparison to other neighborhoods in Oakland but big in heart. Cairo Road a.k.a. Crack Street as we called it, was a million dollar dope turf. Addicts drove through and walked up Crack Street with intentions of purchasing crack rock. This was an every day event, day and night, seven days a week.

I saw how Crack Street was poppin' and how my friends were coming up fast. Guys were 16, 17 years old playing with grown man money. Kids tucking in $50,000 - $100,000 under their mattresses or in shoe boxes. I remember going to a friend's house and he showed me $25,000 that he had in a briefcase. At the time he was 17 and I was 16.

All it took was for me to make a $10 bet on the Super Bowl with a classmate in 1988. I can't even remember who was playing that year, but I remember winning. Instead of a cash payment he told me that he only had dope and would double me up, which simply meant that I would receive $20 worth of crack instead of $10 cash.

A few of my friends were already grinding (selling dope) but I hadn't yet given in to the temptation. Now was as good a time as any, so I took the rock and flipped it, and from that day forward, my life changed. Money came fast, I mean it came *fast*.

Most of my friends dropped out of school once they started getting that dope money, but not me. My grandparents would have murdered me. So in the interest of self preservation, I went to class and got decent grades. That's the difference right there, the effect of a dual parent household on a child's life. Even though I was selling dope, I still respected my grandfather enough to get good grades and finish high school. School was one thing that I couldn't hide, but getting money, at least in the beginning, was easy.

As time passed it became very difficult to hide the money that I was earning. I would post on the turf and drug fiends were everywhere. We would have to yell, "Give me 13 feet!" just to get some personal space. They would back up and almost form a line. It was crazy the things a crackhead would do for a fix.

I always knew that I was doing wrong and that it wouldn't last, but the money had me. It came fast and was spent even faster. I was having a tough time mentally because I wasn't raised that way. I was destroying my people and breaking the law on a daily basis, but the more I sold and the more money I made, the more I rationalized the whole situation. I would tell myself things to justify why I was doing this: *I* might as well get the money because these crackheads are gonna get their drugs from *someone* and it might as well be me. I told myself, "I'm only going to do this for a little while, just to get on my feet." Here's the thing: you never get on your feet, even when you are stacking more money than most people earn in a lifetime. You can never make enough money in the game. That was me.

Money was the goal; money, money, money. What more can I say? It had me risking my freedom and more importantly, my life. Foolish, huh? I felt as if the only way I could support my family and myself was by way of selling drugs. It was a long slippery slope. The longer I sold drugs the easier it became to justify my actions, and eventually there weren't any more justifications needed. This was who I was, period. But the truth of the matter was, I really *wasn't* this guy. I had allowed my circumstances and environment to alter me.

The more I earned, the bolder I got. I really didn't care what anyone thought. All that mattered was the almighty dollar. As I grew financially so did my hood. Everyone down with the cause was earning money, hand over fist. This eventually brought about beef. Any time money is involved, jealousy sooner or later rears its ugly head. Aside from that, my hood was good.

Cars, clothes, and women willing to do whatever I demanded came easy. Spur of the moment flights and vacations were the norm. Las Vegas was my favorite spot. I loved the fast pace of the city and the gambling. I gambled so much at the MGM and Caesar's Palace that they gave me a VIP card that I handed over to the pit boss every time I gambled. I often lost more than I won but it was good because the casinos would comp me things like 5-star dinners and shows - any show I wanted to see. It didn't matter if it was at their casino or not, it was totally up to me. Any club, whether it was on the strip or not, provided VIP benefits with bottle service. I was comped luxury suites when I came to town. I lost a lot of money in Las Vegas and they wanted to keep me comfortable and coming back. But I didn't care; I was young and having fun. Boy, was I stupid!

Gambling is a huge waste of time, energy, and money. Dice games would start all the time on the street but I preferred a more closed and controlled environment, that way I didn't have to worry about anyone robbing the dice game. We would bet $100 and side bet whatever. No matter how much I won in any crap game, I never came close to the amount I lost. How many times have I told myself ,"I wish I knew then what I know now?" But that's life; you live and you learn.

D.D.S. (Dope Dealers Syndrome) is something a friend and I came up with. Simply put, selling drugs makes you lazy! It locks you into a state of mind that has the ability to mislead you. For example, a person suffering from D. D. S. will be convinced that selling dope is all that they can do. Another example is someone walking around with large amounts of money believing that they can buy everything with cash, never understanding the possibilities and power of credit. With the right credit score more options are at your disposal than with just cash.

Life as a drug dealer was very interesting. Everyone wants something from you because most of the people that you are in contact with come from a position of lacking, and that alone can be detrimental to one's health. When people are held back financially, whether it's due to self or the environment that they grew up in, it's bound to be a problem. Some people will do anything for money, even risk their own lives and freedom.

Being a drug dealer was very unpredictable. It had its ups and downs, but if you pay attention, a lot can be learned. The main lesson I learned was survival and self preservation. You also learn the do's and don'ts rather quickly. I noticed the longer I participated in that lifestyle, the less I wanted to accomplish; I didn't want to do anything else but grind (sell drugs). I didn't want to work or do anything productive. Product and profits were all I thought about, and to not let anyone or anything affect my bottom line, which was money. That was my philosophy. I sold to anyone that wanted my product; money ruled my world. My pager would ring incessantly, and nine times out of ten it meant money. The average person works hard at his/her job and then kicks back on the weekend. Every day was my weekend. Selling drugs makes you lazy and over time you begin to think that this is all you can do. I personally know people who are in their 30's, 40's and 50's still grinding and have been for many years. You probably know of someone who lives like this. This isn't just an Oakland thing or even a California thing; this is happening all across the country.

All of those years could have been used in a productive manner to help better their lives. Invest in yourself for the future. I'm not trying to cast anyone in a negative light because that isn't my intention here; I simply want to show how selling dope makes a person lazy and can trap you into a way of life that is unproductive.

Then there is law enforcement, and they are not playing fair. You know why they aren't playing fair? Because contrary to popular belief, it's not a game! So local and federal officials use advanced technology to capture and detain suspects. The law surrounding drug offenses are lopsided and never in the offender's favor. When you get caught, the law is strict and severe, especially federal drug laws which have mandatory minimum sentencing guidelines. For example, 500 grams of powder cocaine is punishable by five years of federal detention, but 28 grams of crack (which is generally sold in predominantly black neighborhoods) is punishable by five years in federal lock up.

I didn't know anything about federal laws or even about the mandatory minimum guidelines that U.S. judges had to abide by. Even if the sentence did not fit the crime the judge had to stick to the guidelines with no deviation. People who dealt drugs were being sentenced to more time for non-violent offenses than murderers and child molesters. To be honest, had I known about these guidelines and laws, I still wouldn't have stopped selling drugs. It would have been just another obstacle in the game. In the words of my late grandfather, "I don't give a rat's ass." Yeah, those words pretty much summed up my state of mind during that period of my life. Money was always the motivating factor for me.

The '80s and '90s were a very unique and dangerous time to live in America as a young black male teenager. They were unique because a young ambitious black male could make large sums of cold hard cash, but there was danger because money breeds greed and envy, which often leads to death. Many young men have lost their lives to the drug trade.

For many, change never happens, partly because most are set in a way of thinking that betrays hope. A sense of hopelessness is a common theme in the inner city. I found hope in making money; unfortunately, I felt the only way to make money was to slang crack rock. Countless others have traveled down this same street.

After about eight years, I was tired of hustling and wanted a way out but didn't know how to do it. I was selling large quantities of dope by this time and if I was going to stop completely, then I needed an equal or larger income to replace what I was making selling drugs. That was the hard part, substituting my illegal income and not knowing or understanding how to earn large sums of legal revenue. I didn't know how I was going to do it; I was tired.

Everyone has their rock bottom and I'm not any different. My rock bottom came in the form of jail. Every drug dealer's nightmare is ending up in prison with a lengthy sentence and mine wasn't any different. The year was 1996, Christmas Day to be exact, when my life changed forever.

I came home to the DEA on my front lawn. Once I saw the three bold letters on the back of their jackets, I knew it was over...or so I thought. Actually, it was just the beginning, the start of a new life. I couldn't see it then as a way out; it was going to cost me everything that I owned.

I was arrested and charged with multiple counts of health and safety violations: possessing more than 10 kilograms of cocaine (Health & Safety. Code, §§11351, 11370.4), possessing cocaine base for sale (id.,§11351.5), and manufacturing a controlled substance (id., §11379.6, subd. (a)).

I was in county lock up awaiting my hearing; man, that was the most depressing period of my life. I was looking at 21 years in a state prison, and if the federal government decided to pick the case up, I was facing 15 years to life under the mandatory minimum sentencing guidelines. I was 26 years old and thought my life was over. The pressure was unreal; I wouldn't wish that type of mental anguish on anyone.

I remember standing before the judge and seeing a look of disgust on her face. The district attorney and my attorney took turns speaking about me as if I was not even in the same room; it was as if I was invisible. I learned a lot about the legal system during this period of my life. Needless to say the judge ruled against me and I was headed to Superior Court to prepare for trail. It was clear to me that I was not going to receive justice. Every judge looked at me with contempt, like they already had their minds made up that I was guilty. I was guilty, guilty as can be, but I thought this was America, the land of the free. You are supposed to be innocent until proven guilty in a court of law, but it appeared to me that the parties involved (the judge and the D.A.) already had their verdicts in, or so I thought.

My fate was in the hands of the judge who knew nothing about me other than what was before him on paper. My lawyer told me, "We literally have one shot in the dark but if we win on this level it becomes easier." I really didn't know or understand the gravity of what he was saying to me, I just wanted to be free. At this point I had been incarcerated for approximately 60 days. My body, mind, and spirit were exhausted. I was tired of thinking about my unknown future and the what if's. What if they give me 21 years? What if they give me 15 years? I went through all of the "what if's" and still hadn't came any closer to some type of peace. I felt hopeless,

hopeless as can be.

I was literally back at square one. All the money that I had saved for years was gone. The sense of security that I felt from amassing a small fortune, the sense of pride and respect that came with the money, the ability to escape my surroundings and environment, was all gone. All I had was me. Little ol' me against the world, with nothing more than my ability to think and visualize.

The pressure was unlike anything I have ever felt before in my entire life. I would think and think, going over any and every scenario. The thought of not knowing the outcome or my future was killing me inside. Jail is a waiting game. My mind and body were tired; I just wanted the whole thing to be over.

I was driving myself crazy. I couldn't find peace; I was a complete mess. I had to be out of my mind because what I did next was pure craziness. I asked any inmate that I came in contact with for meds; Tylenol, Advil, ibuprofen, anything that I could take. I didn't know if I could even overdose from over the counter meds, but I was willing to try. I was really willing to attempt suicide. That was my plan, to end it all.

I didn't want to spend the rest of my life in a cage like some trapped animal. Freedom or death. I was really in pain mentally and that lead to physical pain. Wow, I never ever thought of doing any type of physical harm to myself. Suicide was against everything that I was taught and believed in, but here I was. This was scary for me because I was actually going to go through with it.

The day came for me to do the deed; I had finally acquired enough meds and was ready to go. I was in my cell; I had a one man cell at the time. I was so distraught and nervous. Never in a million years would I have thought that I would be in this situation, but here I was. So many thoughts ran through my mind. Tears ran down my cheeks, then a thought entered my head. The thought was to kneel and pray, ask for forgiveness, and all shall be forgiven. I prayed and cried like a little child.

I instantly felt better. It seemed as if a huge weight had been lifted off of me. I no longer had a sense of hopelessness. No longer was I worried about how much time I would be sentenced to because I knew that God was in the equation now and he had my back.

After the judge heard all of the evidence and remarks from the prosecution and defense, he was ready to make a ruling. It was as if everything had stopped. I was literally hanging on to every word that came from the judge's mouth. My heart was pounding relentlessly, almost jumping out of my chest.

The judge threw the case out, citing that the state violated my rights under the 4th Amendment: *The right of the people to be secure in their persons, houses, papers, and effects, against unreasonable searches and seizures, shall not be violated, and no warrants shall issue, but upon probable cause, supported by oath or affirmation, and particularly describing the place to be searched, and the persons or things to be seized.*

Basically the state needed a warrant before entering my residence, and since they did not have one, the case was dismissed. I was free, let off the hook so to speak...or so I thought. All those feelings of joy and relief ended once my lawyer explained that the prosecution was meeting with the grand jury to seek an indictment. If indicted, I would stand before a superior court judge and my lawyer would submit a motion for dismissal on the grounds of the 4th Amendment. Needless to say, I was, in fact, indicted.

A few weeks later I was standing in front of a superior court judge. My lawyer had submitted a motion for dismissal on the grounds of illegal search and seizure.

He simply stated that my constitutional rights had been violated. The judge agreed, he deemed everything from that search 'the fruit of a poisonous tree' and ordered that everything be returned to me except, of course, the drugs and firearms.

I was released later that evening. It felt unreal; I was in a state of disbelief. Everyone that I had known up to that point that ended up on the wrong side of the law usually stayed there for a while, but I was given a second chance and wasn't about to mess it up. I promised God and myself that from that day forward I would live a legal existence. If I could make it to the heights above the average every day drug dealer and survive on that level and steadily elevate in that career choice, then why couldn't I excel in a legal realm? I told myself I could and never looked back.

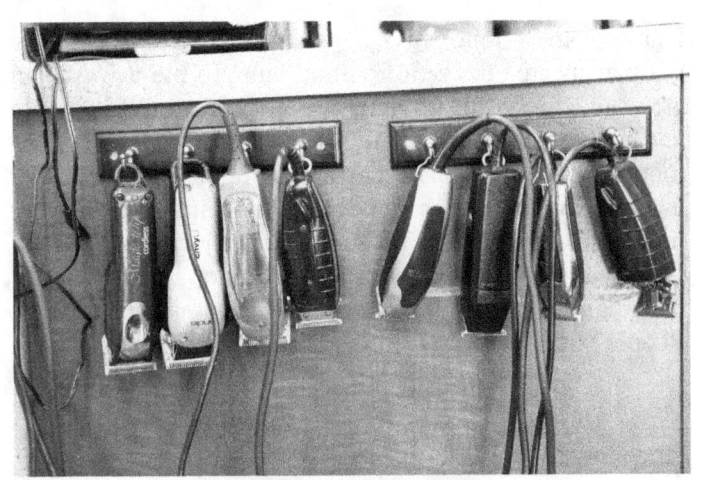

CHAPTER 2

THE ART OF BARBERING

Being a barber is more than just cutting hair. It encompasses many different things that will be called upon at different times. For example, a client might have an issue going on in his or her life that you can help them with, even if it is nothing more than a few kind words. Sometimes you might not have the answers they are searching for, but being respectful and kind will go a long way. Respect is a must in this business; it can make or break you.

My first day of barber college was easy. All I had to do was watch the other students cut hair. That was my assignment for the entire week, which was fine by me because honestly I was a little scared to cut an actual person's hair. The whole week I saw students messing up, but I also saw works of art. To me it was just a haircut; I didn't respect the craft. It was all about getting paid.

I have been cutting hair for twenty years now and

I have come a long way. When I first started I can't say that I respected the art of cutting hair. To me it wasn't an art at all. It represented money, point blank, nothing more and nothing less, and money was the primary motivating factor for me back then. I was looking at being a barber as just a job and not as a career. When things are done for money and purely just for money, a majority of the time it doesn't last because when a problem or situation arises that requires a little thought, it can become too difficult. People usually move on or quit, and that's exactly what almost happened to me.

After my first week, it was time to pick up the clippers and get started. It was rough. It seemed as if no matter what I tried, I just couldn't get it right. Other students would laugh at all my failures. They would stand behind the nearest fan to make it sound like the police and yell into it saying, "Put the clippers down! You are surrounded, I repeat, put the clippers down!" It was hilarious but at the same time embarrassing.

After about a month of barber college, I learned the basics of a good haircut. I was starting to get the hang of it, but for some reason a bald fade was very difficult for me to grasp. A low even cut, a taper, and even a ta-pered Afro was starting to fall into a space of understanding for me but a bald fade seemed nearly impossible for me to master. It might as well have been calculus or learning Chinese. I just couldn't wrap my head around the concept of what exactly went into creating a bald fade. I know it sounds crazy; it's just a bald fade, but there is so much that is involved in creating this cut, as there is in all cuts.

When a client sits in the barber chair and explains how he wants his hair cut, you will need to be able to visualize that style on his head. Sometimes the particular style that the client wants isn't what he should get because the style might not be a fit for his type of hair or shape of head. As a barber, you will need to know how to express that to the client in a manner that isn't damaging to his ego or pride. Barbers shouldn't be overly aggressive and should always be pleasant in nature. This will help in attracting a large clientele base.

Additionally, you have to make sure that the proper amount of hair is cut to ensure the correct length. Someone told me once, "If you cut too much off it can't be put back. But if you cut just a little and let the client tell you to go shorter, then you can never go wrong." My brother William (we call him June) was an apprentice barber in my shop. One day a guy came in for a cut. I had a client in my chair already so he sat in my brother's chair. The guy said, "Cut it all even but do not cut the lower back at all because I'm growing it out." June said, "OK", and started cutting his hair.

June cut and cut until there wasn't anything on the back of the client's head, the exact area the client did not want to be cut. The client was very upset, as he should have been. He walked out without paying for the service. The cut itself was decent, but if that style wasn't what the client wanted, then it is a bad haircut. Even if everyone else says that it looks good, it's a bad cut. What matters the most is what the client thinks and says.

There are exceptions; sometimes a particular style or cut isn't suited for that individual so you have to find a respectful way to convey or express yourself. Every person has their own unique head shape and hair texture; everyone is different, no two people are the same. Still most people want what they see. I can't count how many times someone saw me finishing up a client and said, "I want my hair cut just like that!" It may be the same cut but it may not look the same on a different person.

The ability to visualize is important. As a barber

there are many different times throughout the day that I have to rely on the power of visualization. It is a very powerful tool not only for cutting hair but also in life.

When I was three years old, my grandfather drew a picture of an elephant. I remember asking him to teach me to draw an elephant just like the one that he had drawn. He sat me down and began to instruct me in the fine art of drawing elephants. He taught me to visualize, because without that ability there were nothing but lines on a piece of paper. After I got the elephant down to a science, at least as best as a three year old could draw it, he showed me how to construct cars, trucks, and homes. I continued to push a pencil on paper for years. I got so good at it that when I was in high school, students would pay me to draw their favorite celebrity.

The ability to see something beforehand is priceless, and drawing has afforded me that ability. Before I can draw anything I have to picture the image in my mind then I go to work. That's how I approach cutting hair. Once the client tells me how he wants his hair, I instantly picture that style and then trace that image from my mind onto the client. Some of the best barbers see it before they do it, and I'm no different. Visualization is the key to becoming a great barber.

Barbers are very competitive and there are so many in school training to become licensed barbers. From state to state, city to city, thousands of potential barbers are positioning themselves to earn a living and possibly take some of your clients. You have to constantly stay on top of the craft.

To be a barber you have to be a people person. This is a must. How could you not be? A barber is in constant contact with people. Hygiene and physical appearance must be on point. I have personally witnessed barbers who have lost clients because they did not smell appealing, in fact they smelled appalling. This goes for marijuana as well. Not everyone smokes and to some it could be offensive. I have gained new clients because their former barber reeked of weed and constantly took smoke breaks before or during a haircut. The point is that in order to succeed in this business you need to be good at the art of barbering *and* have a pleasing personality. Also a good barber will do more than what is required; they will go above and beyond the service that is being requested.

Keep in mind that you are serving other people. These people are more than just a payment. They represent future clients because every time someone stops them and asks where they get their hair cut, you want them to say your name or shop. In essence, all clients are walking billboards.

There is a lot of money that can be earned in the hair industry. Great barbers make life changing amounts of money and good barbers have the same potential. Whatever you aspire to be as a barber, there a few things that you will need to know and put into practice. You need to be humble, hungry, and a hustler.

When a person is humble they tend to come off with an air of appreciation that can be seen and felt without actually being voiced. Less pride and more humbleness is always best. I'm not saying that you shouldn't have any pride, I'm just saying that too much can be a terrible thing. Humbleness is pleasing to others. To become a successful barber you will need to be pleasing to other people.

Hunger is the amount of ambition that a person may possess. You have to stay ambitious. Ambition is what keeps me moving towards my goals. Without a true hunger to succeed and to become more in my life, I'll just become comfortable and stagnant. Nothing is wrong with being comfortable but you shouldn't be stuck and blinded by comfort.

Hustle comes easy to some and for others it is a daily ritual. It seems that I come in contact with a lot of people who think that they are hustlers but the truth of the matter is, they are not. To me the definition of a hustler is someone who has the ability to sell something, an item, or anything for that matter, that doesn't sell itself. Many drug dealers claim to be natural born hustlers, but dope sells itself so how can you claim that title?

I have been cutting hair for twenty years and eighteen of those as a licensed barber and owner of my own barbershop, Creative Reflections. Throughout the years I have come across many barbers; some have worked with me in my shop. The number one problem I noticed working with new barbers was they expected something for nothing. They enter into the industry thinking, "I'm a licensed barber in a shop, so I will be making a lot of money." Unfortunately it doesn't work like that. You have to put in the time and work.

No one owes you anything in this business nor in life, but for some reason most people seem to think that society owes them. If you are thinking this, you need to get that thought out of your head. Anything worth having will not come easy or quickly. It takes time to build a successful business. Trust me, if you are a barber then you are a business and like most businesses it will require you to work yourself daily. You might be tired, you might be sick, you might be hurt physically or mentally, but in order to make the business grow you will have to do things that the average person isn't willing to do. This is perfectly OK; that is why they are average and you are not.

Hustle with confidence and hustle hard. Never treat the business of barbering as just a hustle; this is disrespectful to the industry and all of the professional people around the globe. This is not just a hustle, it's a career. You must sell yourself so you can grow.

Gaining clientele is never easy but it is the only way to earn experience and grow as a barber. If you are a fresh graduate from barber college and passed the state requirements to become licensed, congratulations! You have made it to the start of something new and challenging. New because this is a fresh start unlike anything or any job that you have ever worked before, and challenging because you will have to discipline yourself, daily.

There were many days I didn't cut one single head when I first opened my shop. I remember when I first opened my shop, not one person walked in for a service for a whole week. I was confused; I didn't know what was going on. I had at the time a seemingly perfect location. There wasn't another barbershop for at least two miles in all directions, there was plenty of foot traffic and a high school was two blocks down. I just couldn't understand where I was going wrong.

However, I was going about the whole thing incorrectly. It wasn't me exactly, it was something totally different. I was stuck on the thought of me losing my investment, of failure, of what people were going to think, and soon negative thoughts consumed me. I had to drop to my knees and pray for guidance. Once I got rid of the negative thoughts I was feeding myself, I began to think more clearly.

I found a graphic designer and told him that I didn't have too much money but would like for him to design a business card and flyer. He gave me a quote and I quickly realized that I could only afford one, so I went with the fliers. The thought was that I could put the fliers on cars, in mailboxes, and pass them out personally.

The fliers were very simple and straightforward. They included my business address, phone number and a hand drawn picture of a barber behind a chair with the client looking at his cut with a hand held mirror. Even though it was hand drawn, it was made flawless with the help of computer technology.

I was really in a bad situation, or so I thought. I had spent all of my money on a barbershop that wasn't producing an income, so this was my Hail Mary in the final quarter; I had to make it work. I didn't have a safety net. All I had was a mind full of ideas and an ambitious spirit.

My brother and I canvased the neighborhood, putting fliers in as many mailboxes as we could, then we went to all of the local clubs and handed them out there as well. We also put them on the windshields of as many vehicles as possible. I always was in hustle mode and networking mode. I introduced my self to people in line at a grocery store or a mall, which led to me giving that person my flier.

The most overlooked potential client is women. If she doesn't want or need it for herself, she might have kids or a cousin, or maybe even a boyfriend or husband that can be referred. Trust me, it happens. I learned quickly the value of a firm handshake and a genuine smile.

Always looking for more clients to service, I constantly walked around no matter where I was and looked at people's haircuts. However, you just can't walk around looking at people; somebody might get the wrong idea, and some sure enough did, but I would put his mind at ease, explain what I did and gave him a flier. That would be all I needed to get a conversation going and a potential new client. Simple as that. To this day I have the habit of checking out people's haircuts; I'm just a little more discreet these days.

In today's social media environment, there are many different ways to market a business: Instagram, Twitter, Facebook, Snapchat, Periscope, Ustream, and a whole host of blogs and bloggers. Advertising can be very cheap, if not free in many cases. Some of these sites allow you to share your media with other sites. For example, when I take a picture of a haircut that I just completed, I can post it on Instagram and share that same picture simultaneously to Facebook, Twitter, and Tumblr. Different people have stopped by in order to give me a chance at cutting their hair, which is an honor, and they came in all because of my social media marketing.

There are different photo apps that help enhance pictures. There are even some free apps out there but I have learned that the best apps in many cases are the ones that are paid for. I personally use an app called Word Swag. I can edit my photos directly from my phone. Text can be added with different fonts and colors; it is a very powerful tool. The price for Word Swag is $2.99 and is worth every cent.

Once I started marketing through these channels, I noticed an instant change. I started seeing familiar faces as well as some new ones. It wasn't super busy but at least I was earning an income, which was a big motivating factor for me. Honestly, if the advertising hadn't worked then I would have to try something different but I knew that quitting was not an option. Again, I didn't have a safety net. It was all or nothing, so I had to make it work and that's exactly what I have done. I have purchased several pieces of property from the income I've earned as a barber. If I had quit, none of that would have been possible.

My advice to young new barbers is to not get discouraged if things do not start off the way you pictured. Keep in mind that it will take time. Anything worth having will require some amount of work and know-how. Nothing will be handed to you or given to you. Plan for your future. Figure out exactly what it is you want and wake up every morning with plans to make sure that you move towards it. Progress will happen no matter how large or small, as long as you are progressing. Small forward progress is OK but stationary or reverse movement is unacceptable in my opinion. Always move forward.

With forward motion you will inevitably grow. Growth as it relates to a barber can come in many forms. For example, learning a cut that is unfamiliar to you. Maybe you didn't know or understand how to do a certain style or cut so you never tried it. But I'm here to tell you that if the style or cut is learned and mastered, you will open yourself up to more clients and revenue.

Additionally, you will grow and earn a good living if you take care of business. Taking care of business is respecting your clients, being on time, greeting everyone that enters your establishment, as well as many more simple things that can help you achieve success. Many barbers chase the money; there's nothing wrong with that but there are opportunities and growth in making barbering your passion. When you follow your passion, the money will come and usually because of the passion that you display, opportunities will arise. Many different opportunities have come my way because of my work ethic.

I have met people from all walks of life. Some people were in positions to help advance me financially, and others helped me through their experiences and words of wisdom. People have truly enhanced my life. Because of this career, I have had the pleasure of meeting and cutting the hair of lawyers, police officers, federal agents, doctors, educators, real estate brokers and agents, and more. All of these people have enriched my life much more than on just a monetary level.

The bottom line is that people must like and trust you in order for you to advance yourself. Many people have come in to my business because one of my clients referred him or her. I try to make new customers feel comfortable and at ease when at my shop; it is already a nervous situation. Getting a haircut is serious business especially if it is the client's first time in your chair, so some amount of comfort is beneficial.

Plan, plot, and strategize is the movement. This is a very important statement because in order to succeed, a certain amount of planning will need to be done; it's vital. Setting goals for yourself helps you to envision exactly the thing or things that you are trying to accomplish.

Imagine that you are on the phone with a friend that you haven't seen or spoken to in years. There are a lot of memories that both of you reminisce about and discuss. The friend asks you to stop by their home in order to catch up, and you agree. It felt good reconnecting with your friend and you can't wait to see them, but there is just one problem: you didn't get the address. It would be easy to simply call back and get the address but the point that I am trying to make is that you cannot get to a destination without an address or location. Once the location is determined then mapping out a course or route can be determined. Without a route you are just wondering around, lost. Being lost is not a good feeling and most people are wandering around, doing what they see other people doing with no clear direction of their own.

You must plan to achieve the things you want in life, but first you need to know what it is that you want. Knowing exactly what it is that you seek is a very important step to achieving your goals. Thinking about the thing that you wish to have is an important first step. You must pinpoint with accuracy then plan and execute fearlessly. Without knowing what you want to achieve would make planning and executing impossible. You need to be certain or definite on exactly what it is you want.

Once you know exactly what you want, you must make moves *every day* to ensure it comes to fruition. You must follow the plan fearlessly. Fear has held many men back from achieving a higher level of life. I can recall a time in my life when I was fearful but didn't allow my fear to get the best of me. The federal government had just given me back one of my vehicles that they hadn't sold at auction. It was scheduled to be auctioned soon, but a judge had ruled that all my possessions must be given back to me because the charges against me were the "fruit of a poisonous tree".

It was a 1988 Chevy stepside truck. I had done a lot of work to this truck prior to my incarceration. From top to bottom, everything was new. The engine, transmission, candy paint, the interior was authentic leather with a wood grain finish, and of course, it sported a set of chrome rims. I had invested over $40,000 into that truck, so to get it back at that time in my life was a good thing.

I wanted to keep the truck but knew that I couldn't afford it anymore. At that time I was working as a shuttle driver, picking up and dropping off passengers; I hated that job. The pay wasn't good at all. I really wanted to cut hair but didn't have a license. I had completed barber college but hadn't taken the state exam yet, so financially I was a mess. However, this vehicle was just what I needed to start new and fresh.

I sold the truck for $10,000 and the buyer also gave me another truck. I sold that truck for $2,500, giving me a total of $12,500. My old self knew exactly what to do with that type of money - flip it. Keep flipping it until when? Until I ended up in prison or dead? Not me. I had already tried that route and almost ended up with a life sentence, so I began looking for a space to rent or lease for my barber business.

When I finally found a space, I was hesitant because of fear, a fear of failure. I had been working hard at a dead end job that I absolutely hated. In a matter of days I received a vehicle that I sold for cash that I considered start up capital for a barbershop, but yet I was fearful of failing. My mind raced with all types of negative thoughts and almost made me reconsider. My gut was telling me to move forward though, so I secured a lease for the building. That was nineteen years ago, and I still remember the address: 8909 MacArthur Blvd.

I purchased my first home for my family and with the money I earned from that first barbershop. Imagine what might have happened if I hadn't secured the lease because of a fearful mentality. Who knows, but I'm happy that I pushed past my fears. It took every nickel I had to get the building and equipment needed to have a functional and safe barbershop. I did all of this without a barber's license, which was a real concern to me at that time.

Five months after I had opened my shop, I took and passed the state of California barber exam. I was the only one that passed that day. I was ecstatic to say the least. I had studied and studied for the exam, so I was well prepared. I also saw myself passing and knew that I was deserving. I learned a long time ago that I must envision myself reaching a goal and believe that it has happened. I saw myself becoming a barber; not just any type of barber, but a successful barber. That is exactly what I am today.

Sometimes people can be cruel and take their problems out on the world, then bring that negative energy into your business. I have witnessed on countless occasions people coming into the shop upset about whatever is going on in their life and just bring the entire positive energy of the shop down. We could have been having a good time, but that good time was shut down by negative energy.

I have a client who for some reason or another always appeared to be mad. Every time he came in for a haircut he made people feel uncomfortable. Negative energy is contagious just like positive energy. One day it was just him and I in the shop and we had a discussion about his attitude. He hadn't realized the amount of pressure that he was putting on me and the other clients. We worked it out and everything was cool.

As a barber you wear many hats and honestly for all that is required and expected of us, we are underpaid. I say that because you need to have some type of understanding of human behavior; clients expect their barber to be a therapist, and that is just the beginning of expectations: sports analyst, political analyst, religious leader, and guidance counselor are other things you're expected to be well versed in, just to name a few.

One way to acquire a certain amount of understanding of these topics is by reading. Read books and news articles. I remember the day I first picked up a book and read it. A friend of mine suggested that I read *Make Me Wanna Holler: A Young Black Man in America* by Nathan McCall. That was the first time I had ever read a book from beginning to end that wasn't a class assignment. Reading helps expand your way of thinking and sparks the brain unlike anything else that I have experienced. It was once said, "If you want to hide something from black people, put it in a book." I don't know who said this originally, but I highly encourage my people to read more.

The more you have to offer as a barber, the more potential clients will be interested in you as a person. Like I said earlier, people must like you in order for them to spend money with you unless you're the only show in town and that's extremely rare. In every city, there are many barbers. The competition is fierce; you have to stay on top of your game. Sometimes that might mean more education, or information gathering as I like to call it.

Education doesn't necessarily mean going back to school. It could mean something unconventional, such as attending a hair show. The hair shows that I have attended have had courses in a classroom setting. I went to the Bronner Brothers Hair Show once and it was something to see. There were vendors selling their products, and barbers and stylists performing their favorite haircut or style for a captive audience.

The best thing I took away from the experience was meeting different people from so many backgrounds, but they all came together to learn and share knowledge. It was truly an uplifting, educational, and unique moment. At that time I had probably been cutting hair for about fifteen years; sometimes you get stuck in a routine that becomes habit forming to the point, in my case, where you don't want to change. However, I knew something had to change because I was starting to burnout.

I took a class that Ivan Zoot was teaching. At the time I had never heard of him but remember thinking his name was different and kind of funny. It turned out to be the best thing to happen to me at that time in my career because it recharged me. He talked about how everything is costing more and more these days, but the price of a haircut stays the same and how we as barbers are always the last to raise our prices, and that needs to change. He encouraged us to charge more and stay firm in the decision. By not providing discounts to anyone, you will earn more and work less.

He was right. As soon as I started charging more, the cheap people stopped coming in, which eliminated a lot of haggling which I hated doing. Not only did charging more earn me more money but it also gave me peace of mind.

You really have to love what you do, and that goes for anything, not just cutting hair. If you don't love it, I suggest that you find something that you do love. If not, then you are doing yourself a disservice. Work will start to feel like a chore, a drudgery. Being a barber is a very good career. Many undervalue the earnings of barbers but good barbers are the ones buying property and starting side businesses. I know plenty of barbers who are successful, including myself.

In order to gain success as a barber, there are many things that must be in place first. Too many to list in fact, but I am going to give a few that have served me well over the years and have paved the road towards my success. While these examples refer to the barbering profession, they can be applied to just about any career.

1. Maintain a clean safe environment. This is a must; the shop has to be clean not only for appearance purposes but also for health reasons. The last thing you want is for someone to become sick from being in your establishment. There is always hair and dust piling up in little places throughout a barbershop. Make sure that your station and chairs are clean. Clients shouldn't have to sit in a dirty chair with other client's hair still in it. Also, clean the tools that are being used. This goes a long way in building a barber-client relationship. I know first hand because the majority, if not all, of my clients have told me at some point how much they appreciate me cleaning my clippers between each client. I know of some barbers who clean their clippers once, maybe twice a day. That's totally unacceptable! I clean after every client; it takes a little bit more time but none of my clients have bumps or any type of infections growing around or in the back of their head. A helpful thing to do from time to time is to sit in the waiting area and observe the surroundings, this way you can see exactly what the client sees. If what you see isn't appealing because of unsightly debris or dirt and trash, then clean, clean, clean. Oh, did I mention clean? I'm stressing the importance of a clean environment because not only is it a state board requirement in California, but you should want your customers and potential customers to enjoy a clean safe establishment.

2. Maintain a pleasing personality. If people don't like you, then guess what? They won't spend their hard earned cash with you. It is important that you are a people person. Speak to people as they enter and exit the shop. A simple, "Hello, how are you doing today?" when someone enters, or a grateful, "Thank you, have a good day!" when they leave can go a long way in building relationships and clientele. If you aren't a people person then I suggest you do one of two things. One, work on becoming a people person or two, get a job working in another profession because a job dealing with people isn't for you. The odds are against you because you will deal with people daily. That's where the money is coming from: people.

3. Do more than what is required. Doing just the bare minimum will get you minimum pay. Always make an attempt to go above and beyond the expectations of a normal barber. Make the client feel special. Sometimes that may require a little more effort or just some flattering kind words, but only if you really mean it. The right words at the right time can have a positive effect, but the same words at the wrong time can be detrimental. This is why being a people person is mandatory. A barber that has a basic understanding of his client's needs will excel.

4. Be grateful. Gratitude is a must! Nobody owes you anything, so when people come and spend their hard earned money at your business, thank them and be sincere. After every cut, I let that client know that I really appreciate him or her and their business. They are contributing to supporting me and my family. Saying the words *thank you* is pleasing to hear and it makes people want to come back to you. No one wants to give their money to an ungrateful person. Keep in mind that you're not the only barber in town. If you are the only barber in town, even then you should show an appreciative spirit.

One day I wanted to do something to show my appreciation to all of my clients. I bought donuts and had them available for anyone to enjoy. I did that for about a week or so. The problem was, most people didn't want any and at the end of the day I was stuck with a half dozen donuts. Then I tried pizza, and the same thing happened. I really wanted to show my clients that I did in fact care about them and wanted to demonstrate this on a personal level. I was aiming to make a connection with my clients that they probably never had experienced before. Then it hit me: I will text every client whose phone number I had in my contact list. If I didn't have someone's number, I ask for it. That was different right there because usually if the client likes your work he or she would ask for your number or card, so by asking for the client's number, I was already set apart from most barbers.

I sent out "thank you" text messages when I got home after work. I tried sending them throughout the day but it proved to be difficult for me because of the high volume of clientele that was constantly coming into the shop. I sent out each message one by one, personalizing each and every one so they knew that the message was just for them.

5. Be knowledgeable. As a barber, I learned early on that in order to really be an asset to my clients I needed to know more. Not just about hair cutting and everything related to it, but also about more general things such as politics, sports, relationship issues, and many more. Honestly there are too many to name, but just understand that by connecting on some type of level with your clients, they will grow to trust you, granting you the possibility of a lifelong client relationship. And, if they're happy with their haircut, that's even better. As a barber you will be required to wear many hats so stay informed and educated in as many areas as possible. You don't have to be an expert in everything, but general knowledge on a variety of subjects is helpful not only to the client but to yourself as well.

6. Know your craft. A chef isn't a chef if he doesn't know how to cook. The same can be said about being a barber. A really good barber knows how to cut many different hair styles, and if he is unfamiliar with a certain cut or style, he will familiarize himself with it. A barber must evolve with the times; haircuts and styles come and go. The Mohawk is a good example of a style that was popular back in the day then became unpopular. Now it is back in the mainstream. The South of France style cut caught on soon after the popularity of the Mohawk dwindled. This particular cut is a variation of the Mohawk, but if you can't cut a Mohawk it would be difficult for you to cut a South of France.

Each and every person that you service is a walking billboard. A large number of my new clients are referrals. They walk in and ask, "Who is Dre?" or, "Does a Dre cut here?" Word of mouth is a good way to build clientele and business, and it means that you are doing something right.

7. Save and invest your money. Saving money is a must! But saving alone is not all that will be needed. It's good to save money that you have earned but there has to be a purpose. It is important that you know exactly what you are trying to accomplish. Without a plan, it can become difficult to just save money and watch it accumulate and not spend it. I found it easier to save money knowing that I was achieving a specific goal.

CHAPTER 3

SAVINGS

For some people, finding a job can be challenging, but do not let those circumstances stop you from gaining employment. It is your God given right to earn a living and be a successful and contributing member of society.

If seeking a job proves to be a task too difficult, then maybe you should think about starting a business of your own. People launch businesses every day, so why not you? First, figure out what you would like to do, then plan for it. Some things might require you to attend a trade school, but you need to find something that you can see yourself doing as a career, something that you enjoy.

That is exactly what I did when I enrolled in barber college. It was a nine month program that required 1,500 hours of training. I didn't know much about cutting hair but at the time it seemed like an easy fit for me. When I was in high school, I cut my own hair as well as a few friends of mine from time to time but only low even cuts, no fading whatsoever, so I had to learn everything associated with barbering. It took time for me to learn all the different styles and hair textures, what tools to use for different people and styles. It was rough in the beginning. I felt like giving up and almost did on many occasions, but I didn't because I knew that in order to effectively change the course of my life I would have to endure some challenges. Not only that, but my friends and family were watching; I wanted to be the example that they looked up to and say to themselves, "If he can do it, so can I."

I forged ahead and never looked back. A few months after I graduated, I took the state exam. I was a nervous wreck. On that day there were only five of us who actually showed up for the test. I don't know if more were scheduled and just didn't come or what, but I was well prepared. All of those days of hard work, studying, and practicing was about to come down to one test. After hours of testing I was the only one that day that passed. I was officially a licensed professional barber.

I opened my barbershop in 1997. After twenty minutes of thought, I named it Creative Reflections and I am still the owner and operator of that business today. If I can do it, so can you! It doesn't have to be barbering - maybe you like working on cars or cooking for the family. Whatever it is, take the first step toward changing your life and the lives of those around and close to you.

Once you start working and have a steady income, you will need to put aside twenty percent or more of each paycheck. I say twenty percent because that is what I started with, but start with whatever you feel comfortable putting aside. It was easy for me to save money because as a barber, I deal with being paid cash daily. I found it easy to save money every day as opposed to a bi-weekly paycheck. This may not be the case for you, and that's okay. Do what works best for you.

Also, I don't have a huge overhead. Each day I saved money earned from the first haircut of the day for a week, then on Monday I would deposit the money into my account. After a year of doing this, I had accumulated a substantial amount. It felt good, and that feeling made me want more so I continued to save.

A really good way to save without using much effort is to 'save the savings'. Save the savings sounds like some type of supermarket sales pitch that you might see on a television commercial and while it's similar, it involves you taking action. How? All you have to do is shop. That's right, *shop*. Every time a receipt is handed to you, do not throw it away. Instead, check out how much the savings were on the discounted/sales items you purchased. *Save* the amount of the savings; put it up and actually save it! Savings! Saving prepares you for investing in the right opportunities.

Don't just stop there with the savings from trips to Walmart, Target, and supermarkets. Apply the strategy to as many different financial situations as possible. Say for example you hire a landscaper to keep the grass cut nice and neat. The landscaper bills you $60 a month. Then one day you purchase a lawnmower at Home Depot with intentions of servicing your own lawn. The lawnmower was on sale – discounted $50 from the original price of $150. Not only do you pocket the $50 savings but you also eliminate the monthly $60 fee paid to the landscaper. Pay yourself $60.00 every month along with all the other savings that you accumulate. Continue to 'save the savings' and watch how much it will grow in a short period of time. Now, you might be tempted to go shopping. Do not! I repeat, *do not* because if you do, all would be lost and all the sacrifices you took were for nothing. Any time you do something differently, it may appear to be difficult but stay focused and keep your eyes on the prize.

Every time I purchase an item, I put the savings away if it was discounted. I'll look for discounts and expect one if an item isn't on sale. It doesn't hurt to ask the cashier for a discount. All he/she can say is no. But what if the answer is yes? I'm always asking when I get to the cashier, "Hi, can I have a discount?" Most of the time the answer is no but sometimes I strike gold. Also, do comparative shopping. For example, I went to a shoe store in the mall. The shoes I wanted were on sale for $119 but they didn't have my size. Across the hall was another shoe store, and the same shoe was $140. I asked to see the shoe in my size. The salesman came back with my size but the price was $21 more for the same shoe in the other store. When I got to the cashier I explained the situation and he agreed to give me the shoes for $119, a savings of $21 that I paid myself. I do this with everything: work done on my home, car repairs, car parts, tires, any and everything that is being sold. If I can get a price reduction, then why not? Once I receive the reduction, I pay myself. I save that money for a week then deposit those funds into a special savings account that is just for this type of activity. If you save the savings and also pay yourself at least 20% of your earned income (money that you earn from working), you will be pleasantly surprised at how much you accumulate in a year's time. Imagine doing this for five or ten years! After the first year, it should become second nature; easy as 1, 2, 3.

What I am about to discuss is for the truly motivated and well disciplined, because it will take both attributes to complete this task. The following is a way to get out of debt faster.

Say you have a car loan and the monthly payment is $500, and you also have a Home Depot credit card debt of $1,500 of which you pay $300 a month (you

46

may be doing this in order to pay off the debt in five months because they offered six months interest free if it was paid in full within that time period. After the six months, interest will be applied at a rate of 19% or more, so it only make sense to pay before interest is applied.).

After you finish paying the Home Depot card off, you might feel a sense of relief; you just paid off a credit card debt and avoided interest. That's a huge accomplishment, but before you go patting yourself on the back and spend the extra cash (the $300 monthly payment) on miscellaneous items, remember that you still have a car loan of $500 a month. What if you increased the monthly payments for your car loan by $300 so that your monthly payment towards that debt is $800? By paying the extra $300 towards the principal, the loan will be paid back sooner, and the faster the loan principal is paid, the less interest you will pay as well. No principal, no interest.

Once the credit card debt and car loan are paid in full, do not go and get yourself back in debt again. Instead *pay yourself.* That's right, pay yourself! I am a firm believer in this. Stop being a consumer and a slave to brand names. Save the $800, but don't just save it. You need to have a purpose. Saving without a goal in mind is a disaster waiting to happen. You are basically hoarding money and as soon as something shiny and cute comes along, the money will be spent; that's a waste of time and money. But if you know and understand your purpose, whatever it is you are trying to achieve, then it's easier to stay on course.

I recommend starting something that will put your money to work for you. Real estate is a great way to create income, whether it's a flip (a home bought with intentions of selling for a profit) or renting to someone else. Put away your money with a purpose, a goal in mind. I'm sure you've heard the saying, "He who fails to plan, plans to fail." That statement is the absolute truth, so plan and strategize like your life depends on financial success. And actually it does.

I suggest that you put the money you save in an interest bearing account. All banks offer savings accounts. Interest bearing is a term used to simply describe accounts that accrue interest. Trust me, the money that you worked hard for is better in a bank than a shoe box or under your mattress, not earning anything. Your money can make you money!

Remember your goal is to earn a certain amount of money in a specific time frame. Cash is king so you will have to have some ready to go when the time is right. Before I purchased my first home I had to go through all of these steps. The thing that kept me focused was accomplishing my unshakable desire to own a home. I couldn't get away from the thought. I had never owned a home before; I always rented, but the benefits were undeniable.

You gain tax advantages when owning a home. As a renter there aren't any tax advantages but your landlord will surely gain. The interest paid on a home mortgage in most cases is tax deductible. Try finding a deduction from rent paid. You can't. Another benefit is the ability to use equity as you see fit. So what is equity as it relates to a home? The answer is simple. Equity is your share of the value of your home, the percentage of the home that you truly own. And here is the best part, you can borrow against the equity that is yours. Let's say you have $100,000 equity in your home. You can borrow sixty-five to seventy percent of that. You will eventually have to pay it back but you can do whatever you want with that cash - buy another home, a new car, or whatever you desire.

***

Retirement Plans/IRA's

Individual Retirement Accounts, or IRA's, are essentially savings plans that assist you in saving for retirement and is a good way to put away money for those golden years of your life. It also has huge tax breaks. With a traditional IRA, you receive a tax break but taxes will not be eliminated; they will be deferred, meaning that taxes are not paid until you make withdrawals. At the age of 59 ½ you can start to take distributions, or withdrawals. Eventually the funds will be taxed but not while it is growing, with interest on top of interest, or "compound interest". If you withdraw funds before age 59½, you will be penalized in the form of taxation.

Most people tend to think that an IRA is an investment, but it really is not. An IRA is simply a method to save money while investing in stocks, bonds, mutual funds, and other investment instruments. Basically you pick which assets to funnel your money into. The money that you put into an IRA is called a contribution and there are limits on the amounts that can be contributed.

Over time an IRA account will be a huge advantage for anyone. The more you contribute, the more money will be compounded with interest throughout the years. I recommend making the maximum contribution each year so upon retirement you can enjoy the maximum financial benefit. The last thing anybody wants is to retire without a sizable nest egg.

There are several types of IRA's. It is important that you talk to someone who specializes in this area. An IRA can be purchased at a bank, credit union, insurance companies or brokerage firms, and they can help you as well by explaining in detail exactly what the pros and cons are.

CHAPTER 4
CREDIT

Credit is a big part of buying a home. There is a credit scoring system in place that is used to determine a debtor's worthiness for a loan and FICO (Fair Isaac and Company) is the system. Without a decent FICO score, it's virtually impossible to obtain a loan. Cash is king but if, like most of the population, you do not have hundreds of thousands of dollars in cash laying around, credit is a form of using other people's money (banks and lending institutions) to purchase things. This is where your credit history is crucial.

A credit score is a numbered rating based on an analysis of a person's debt that represents the risk of lending that person money. A person's credit score is based on credit report information sourced from credit bureaus - the big three are Equifax, Experian, and Transunion.

How does someone go about improving their credit score? The answer is simple and yet complicated all at the same time. Simple because if you do the things that are required, the process can be easy. Complicated because, well, life happens and money is a big part of the equation. You will need money in order to pay off debts. Depending on how bad your credit score is, or if you have ever had credit, will determine the level of complexity. Different things are factored into a person's credit worthiness; each case is different.

First you will need to obtain a credit report from all three credit agencies. This will show your spending history, late payments, and creditors (companies or people that you owe). To obtain a copy of your credit report, contact all three of the bureaus. They all have websites (transunion.com, experian.com, and equifax.com) to make it easy to request your credit history reports.

It is very important to have good credit. Everything is based on your score: loan approvals, loan interest rates, and terms of a loan. Without a decent FICO score, you basically have to use cash as payment. Cash is good, but it will only get you as far as the amount you have; with credit the possibilities are limitless.

Once you receive a copy of your credit report, it is time to get to work. Check for any discrepancies. Contact all three of the credit bureaus and dispute any and all negative items you believe to be incorrect. It is worth noting that the three bureaus do not work together so you may have a negative issue on one or even two of the bureaus but not the other. It is best to contact all three and dispute all discrepancies.

My credit was not good by any means, mainly because of my ignorance as a youth and a reckless regard for credit. I always purchased with cash. Honestly, I never knew of such a thing as credit and how it could affect your quality of life from a financial standpoint. So there I was, 28 years old with bad credit due to poor decision making. I thought if I wanted something I could just buy it with cash. I would have rather rented than owned. The thought of owning a home was beyond my logic at the time. The thought of buying a home seemed stupid. Why spend so much money on a home when I could just pay first, last, and a security deposit? I mean that's how everybody's been living so that's just the way it is. Boy, was I wrong. That's how you live if you settle in that way of life. Trust me, you will miss out on so much by not owning property. It creates options for you and your family.

Once I received my credit report, I went to work on improving it. I immediately contacted my creditors and negotiated settlements with each one. Some were about to fall off (after seven years the debt is dropped) so I did not bother contacting those creditors. If for some reason the debt hadn't cleared after the seven year period I would contact the credit bureau that reported it. If all three, then I would notify all three of them. Once it had been verified then the negative mark would be removed.

Once your credit history is cleared of all negative marks, you can start to build. Keep in mind that no credit in some instances is worse than bad credit, and too many inquires into your credit worthiness can damage your credit as well. A credit card company verifying your information in regards to your credit worthiness is an inquiry.

Obtaining a secured credit card is a quick and simple way to improve and build your credit score. You will need to open an account with a certain dollar amount, and that amount will be used as collateral to secure the card. Whatever bank you bank with should have a secured credit card application. If you do not have a bank account, I suggest that you open one ASAP.

Remember, the goal is to build your score so that a lending institution will be comfortable lending you money.

When opening a secured credit card account, annual fees may apply depending on the institution that you bank with. The amount deposited equals your credit limit, which is the maximum you may charge on the credit card. Payments are not deducted from your account. A statement will be mailed to you and it is your responsibility to pay it on time. Your payment information will be reported to the three major credit bureaus. Positive information will help boost your credit and negative information will harm it, so it is in your best interest to make payments on or before due date. Negative information is obviously counterproductive.

After a year or so of good payment history, you may become eligible to upgrade to an unsecured credit card, maybe even without an annual fee. If you are approved for unsecured credit then at that point the funds that were used to secure the credit card will be refunded.

I was a member of a credit union and went through them for a secured credit card. The process is fairly simple. I just walked into the credit union and asked for an application. Every month I would buy something - shoes, clothes, dinner at a restaurant, anything. When the credit card statement came I paid the full amount due. The card only had a $500 limit but I never spent over $150.

Why wouldn't I charge more than $150 when my limit was $500? The answer is simple. No more than 30% of the credit available on that card should be charged. This process is referred to as *credit utilization*. It is the ratio of credit card balances to credit limits. It is better to have a low credit utilization to help ensure a positive rating. This will show that you're only using a small portion of the credit that has been loaned to you. If you use more or the whole amount on the card, it is considered desperation, so stay at 30% or under.

Another way to boost your credit score is a secured loan, which are offered by many banks. Just like a secured credit card, you are borrowing against a bank account for a certain amount. For example, say you want to borrow $1,000 and have an account with that amount. The bank will use that account to secure the loan. If you really want to positively affect your score, I recommend opening two or three types of this sort of loan, but at different banks, but don't over do it. You don't want to put a strain on your finances. The point of this is to boost your credit status to a point where you will be able to take advantage of different financial instruments. This type of secured loan combined with the secured credit card will elevate you and your credit score to another level, and through these channels you will be able to elevate yourself to a richer, more fulfilling way of life. Banks typically report this type of loan to the credit bureaus, so pay on time and finish off the loan by the due date. This will show a positive payment history.

I also purchased a fairly new vehicle. This creates another loan for which you will be responsible. By showing that you can handle your financial situation properly, you will be improving your credit rating. Keep in mind that you must be able to afford the line of credit that has been extended to you, so some type of employment is necessary. It would be unrealistic to think that you could obtain or even maintain any amount of credit without a steady flow of income.

Employment is a large component of realizing the goal of earning major revenue. If maintaining a steady job is an issue with you at the moment, maybe working a 9 to 5 is not your thing. Starting a business of your own might be the solution. Whether it's a traditional job or self employment, you will need a steady flow of income. Honestly, no institution will lend you any amount of money without some type of way to gain a return for their buck. Would you loan someone money knowing that person is unable to repay the loan? Of course you wouldn't.

Credit is very important and can either enhance your life or become a nuisance. Bad credit can ruin you on a financial level. We sometimes need credit in order to purchase things when we don't have the cash to buy something outright, such as big ticket items like homes, boats, and cars. Usually these things are purchased with credit, unless you are a millionaire and have access to that type of cash. Even millionaires use credit; it's called using other people's money. That's one of the reasons why a millionaire is wealthy - they don't spend their own cash, they use other people's money. Protect your credit; money and credit go hand in hand.

Sometimes you can make a mistake - they can and will happen, but they can be overcome. In 2006 we began to look for another home, something bigger than what we had, to buy and move into. After about a month or so we found what we thought was the perfect house for our family's needs - more square footage and close to highways and our jobs. I submitted an offer and the owner accepted it. The asking price was $395,000. After closing costs and taxes, the total price of the house was approximately $412,000. I wrote a check for a little more than $90,000, which was slightly more than a 20% down payment. This amount down guaranteed that I wouldn't have to pay PMI (PMI, or Private Mortgage Insurance, is explained in more detail on page 71).

The real estate market was hot at that time. There wasn't a property in Oakland that wasn't expensive. A fixer (a home that is not in move-in condition) was upwards of $300,000. People were overbidding on properties because lenders and underwriters were basically signing off on loans for one hundred percent financing without real proof of earned income, so a person could have good credit and buy a house without putting any money down and be approved. Many home owners began to refinance their homes, and many abused the system. They treated their home as a personal ATM. This helped create a climate that eventually caused the market to crash and burn. People were losing and walking away from their homes left and right. It was a very difficult time in not just real estate but in the financial world as a whole. It seemed as if every financial institution was affected by the real estate melt down crisis. Many homes were worth less than what they initially sold for. 'Upside down' or 'under water' were the terms used to describe these situations.

My home was upside down as well, but I knew that I wouldn't lose any money unless I sold my home. That wasn't an option for me at the time so I didn't worry about it. However, one day I noticed a change in my neighborhood. I started to see more people hanging out on the street that I lived. I didn't really think anything of it at first, but then the next day it was the same thing and becoming worse. People were everywhere, up and down the block; it became an every day thing. The block became a dope turf literally overnight.

It was starting to become a big problem. Drug addicts were standing in front of my house. I would come out of the comfort of my home to ask them to move. "Keep it moving" became my mantra. I said it so much that I had dreams about it. I never had an issue with reminding people to not stand in front of my house but it wasn't just me I needed to worry about; I had a family to think about.

My son Tobias would run upstairs to our bed-room, scared because he saw shadows and heard voices by his window; he would sleep with my wife and me because he was so afraid. It was turning into a really bad situation. In 2008, we had a beautiful baby girl, and Andreya was welcomed into our family. It has always been my responsibility to make sure that my family was safe and secure, but with the addition of Andreya, a safe and sound home inside as well as outside was even more important. The inside of our home was very much safe and sound, but the outside was a completely different scenario.

I grew tired of the situation that we were living in. The loud noises that constantly went on outside of my front door, people yelling and arguing at all times of the day and night, was more than a nuisance and the home I purchased was no longer worth the price I paid for it. Something had to be done.

I went to the bank that held the mortgage to my home in hopes of a loan modification. Many people were walking away from their properties and banks all across the country were modifying loans. I just wanted to get the mortgage down to what the market rent was at that time so I could rent it to someone and move my family somewhere else. Simple plan, right?

I had been with this particular bank for several years so they had all of my financial information and history. I didn't have to bring in anything except my identification and ATM card. The banker pulled up all of my information then told me that I wasn't eligible for a loan modification because I didn't meet the requirements: I didn't have a "hardship". A hardship could be anything from me or my wife losing employment to the mortgage adjusting, making the new payment unaffordable. I didn't want to walk away from my property like so many others were doing. I just wanted a modification so I could keep the property and rent it out. I left the bank in a fog but quickly came up with a plan that was in the best interest for me and my family.

My credit score at the time was 812, a great score. Many banks and lending institutions would bend over backwards to do business with me, and I had money in the bank, so why not buy another home for my family to move into? That's exactly what I did, and the wife and I began searching for a new home.

I kept up the mortgage payments and paid on time as usual. We decided to buy a nice two story home, twice the size of the one we were living in. We purchased from a real estate developer and our home was to be built from the ground up. I really liked the thought that my family and I would be the first to do everything in the home, that was huge to me. Every house I had purchased had been pre-owned. I remember buying one house that was built way back in 1892, well over a hundred years old. I can only imagine the things that had taken place in that residence throughout the years.

The asking price was $320,000. Again, I wrote a check for 20% to avoid PMI. They broke ground and six months later we had a brand new home. When we moved in, I stopped paying the mortgage on the home we had moved from.

I do not recommend that anyone not pay their debts. In my case however, I needed to move my family from a potentially dangerous situation. The neighborhood was getting worse and worse daily and I didn't want to raise my kids under those bad circumstances. I feel every man has an obligation to protect and provide for his family, and moving away from the hood was my way of protecting my wife and kids. However, in doing so, my credit suffered but I'd rather have a suffering credit score than a suffering family any day.

After I stopped paying the mortgage, my credit score went from 812 to 551, but I didn't care. I was satisfied with my income as a barber and the real estate investments that I had in place. I had savings, income property, and a thriving business. Even with all of that in place for me, credit was still a necessity.

Credit is a very important component to building wealth. It's the key to obtaining the things in life that can increase your financial worth. I knew this at the time but I just needed to get my family in a safe environment. I did not want my kids growing up in an unsafe area; my son was twelve years old and I know firsthand how the environment that you are in can be influential. We moved to a nice suburban town where people actually spoke to us and the sidewalks were painted pink. There wasn't any graffiti on the walls or sidewalks. I woke up in the morning to birds chirping; it was the best place to raise a family.

I am so thankful for all that God has allowed me to accomplish. I managed to change my family's surroundings for the best. Where I come from, most men weren't sticking around to even help take care of their kid(s). My kids have always been a number one priority, so to pull us out of a ghetto situation and into a suburban lifestyle is truly a blessing and a major accomplishment that I am proud of.

Eight months had passed since I stopped paying the mortgage for the house in Oakland before the bank finally agreed to allow me to short sell it. If you owe more on the mortgage of a home than what the home is actually worth, it can be sold if the bank approves a short sale. They wanted a hardship and I gave them one by not paying the mortgage. The property sold fairly fast but it sold for half of what was owed. I didn't have to worry about the Oakland property anymore and that was all right with me.

I began writing this book with the hope of

helping people. Clients come into the barbershop all the time asking for advice on different subjects, but the most commonly asked question is, "How do I buy a house?" Most of my clients know my story, know that I own income property. I have advised several of my clients throughout the years to their benefit on a variety of subjects, including credit. Different people have told me that I should write a book, so here I am, making my attempt.

A few months into writing this book, I thought, "How can I give advice on credit when mine is bad?" so I began to once again apply the different steps outlined in these pages to my own situation. I ordered my credit report and the main thing on it was the short sale; it was reported as settled for less than full amount due. A short sale is, for obvious reasons, considered derogatory. I couldn't do much about that; I would just have to wait for it to fall off, which usually takes about seven years. I started by opening an account for a secured Visa credit card at my bank. I started with a $1,000 deposit. Since my credit limit was $1,000, I was careful not to charge more than 30%. I didn't want to give the impression that I was living off of the credit card because that could hurt my credit, not help it. I would purchase things such as shoes or maybe take my family out for a nice dinner. When the statement came I made sure that it was paid on time and in full. I then went and opened another account for an secured loan for the amount of $1,000 but at a different bank. Once the paperwork was completed and the money was in the account, I withdrew the $1,000 and every month I would use it to pay back the loan. That way it isn't a financial strain to make the payments. This is done solely for the purpose of building your credit. Secured loans and secured credit cards are just a few of the many different ways to help assist you to bettering your credit score.

After only ten months of making timely payments, my credit score went from 551 to 687, not bad for such a short period of time. Keep in mind that I still had that short sale on my credit report. If I can gain 136 points in my credit score with a derogatory item attached, imagine what yours could be without any derogatory items if you work the principles within this book.

All the different things that I have done to improve my credit score I had done years before, which is how I earned a credit score of 812. I have no doubt that if you follow these proven techniques that you will elevate your score as well. I felt that since my score had dropped that this was the perfect opportunity to test these techniques, and I'm glad that I did because it proves that this information is of value. As of today, my credit score is 740 and rising.

I decided to refinance one of my properties and pull out some money, just to have a little extra cash cushion. That's cash back to *me*. My wife and I needed new vehicles. My car that I used to commute to work was causing me problems and I figured I could refinance to not only get a lower interest rate, but with the extra money we would purchase new cars.

I got the process started with a bank that I already had a relationship with. The process started smoothly but then I ran into troubled waters. The problem was the short sale; it was still on my credit report and most likely would remain for another three years. Banks and lenders see foreclosures and short sales as a problem; it all comes down to your credit worthiness. The higher the score the better, and a low score will almost always result in a denial.

The loan officer at the bank explained that a Letter of Explanation, or an L.O.E., would be required if the refinancing was to be approved. They wanted an explanation as to why I had stopped paying the mortgage, so I wrote a letter explaining my situation.

The circumstances surrounding the short sale were different than most other people's situations. The majority of people who abandoned their homes did so mainly because of some type of financial reason. I had a couple of reasons; safety issues, and my refusal to allow my family to live under the conditions that had become an reality for the neighborhood. It became so bad that I wouldn't allow my kids to go outside and play. Additionally, the banks wouldn't grant a loan modification unless I had a hardship. The plan was to receive a loan modification and rent the property at market value, so the rent received could pay the mortgage and maybe earn a profit at the same time.

In the letter, I explained how the neighborhood had changed and as a result my family didn't feel safe. I grew up under these conditions in my neighborhood, so to me it was nothing more than just life in Oakland but I had to consider that I had a family to protect. If something happened to any one of my immediate family members, it would have been impossible for me to forgive myself because I was in a position to change the environment that we lived in.

After I submitted the L.O.E., the loan officer told me that it was now up to the underwriter, the one who denies or approves the loan after evaluating risk. My credit wasn't exactly the best but it for sure wasn't bad, and about six weeks later I was approved and money was funded to my account.

Again, good credit is very important in today's society. Not having good credit can make life difficult, but using credit correctly can make a profound difference in your life. It's the difference between owning a home in a good neighborhood and living in the slums. Credit, when used properly, can change life for the better.

CHAPTER 5
REAL ESTATE

Real estate is a tried and true method to gain riches when done the right way. No matter where you live in America, I can almost guarantee that there are homes, empty lots, and abandoned houses in your area. Take advantage of your environment. How? The answer is simple, and by investing in real estate you can change your whole life in the process.

America, the home of the free, the land of the brave! America has also been the wealthiest country on the face of the planet for some time, so if you own real estate in the United States of America you in essence own a piece of the richest country in the world, a piece of the American pie so to speak. In order to claim your piece of that pie you will need to have a few things in place, such as good credit and some type of employment. These elements are a necessity for you to reach the goal of becoming a home owner. Through home ownership you can begin to build proper wealth, whether you are buying for a place to live, income property, or with the intention to flip (purchase a property with intentions to sell).

***

Obtaining a Loan

Once you have your credit in order, a loan can be obtained. I know this might seem like a difficult process, especially if you've never obtained or even applied for a loan before. You might think, "What am I getting myself into?" Keep in mind that this process is designed for you to reach your financial goals. The right loan for the right property can change your life.

Get all your documents together - pay stubs, tax returns, and bank statements. These documents are a must in order for a fair assessment of your credit worthiness. This will help you to obtain accurate quotes and pre-approvals.

Shop around for the best deal for your situation. Remember that everyone's situation is different, so never judge your predicament based on someone else's experiences. The best deal is more than just a low interest rate; you should hunt for the best overall loan terms. Finding an honest lender is also key. Unfortunately, when large sums of money are involved some may try to employ unscrupulous tactics, and the field of real estate is not any different.

Once you find a reliable and honest lender, fill out a formal loan application. It is important that you understand all the information that you are submitting. Do not lie under any circumstances. Give only truthful answers. Any fraudulent information can be considered a crime and punishable by the fullest extent of the law. If there are things that you do not understand, ask questions, and ask as many questions as you need so that you are comfortable and fully aware. This is a huge milestone in your life. You do not want to be stuck in a bad loan, so make sure that you exercise due diligence.

During the time you are applying for a loan, do not apply for any new credit cards or lines of credit. That could undermine the initial loan that you are applying for. Once completed, your loan application goes to an underwriter. A underwriter determines if lending money to a borrower is financially feasible. Sometimes he/she will have additional terms. However, it is always up to the underwriter if a loan is approved or declined.

Once you are approved for a home loan, you will have a "pre-approved amount". That amount is the limit that the lender is basically comfortable with lending you. It is based on your income, credit history, and DTI (or debt to income ratio, is explained in more detail on page 69) but can change as your situation changes. That can be for the best or the worse. I suggest that while you have been pre-approved for a home loan that you do not do anything financially irresponsible because that can hurt the pre-approval amount or the whole loan amount itself. Remember, nothing is written in stone until all documents are finalized in closing (when title transfers from seller to buyer).

Additionally, do not be discouraged with the amount that you're approved for if it isn't enough to pur-chase your dream home. At least you have a foot in the door. There are many people who don't get approval for whatever reason. Be thankful and work with what you have for the moment. I have witnessed people losing hope on attaining a home because they weren't approved for a certain amount to purchase a nice home in a nice area. For example, one of my clients was approved for $240,000 but the area that he wanted to purchase based on the comps (the value of homes in an area) were start-ing at $400,000. The only area that he would have been able to buy was in the hood or so far away from his job that the daily commute didn't make sense. To make matters worse, property values began to rise and real estate investors started buying many homes in the hood for income properties. My client eventually gave up and decided to wait it out. What he was waiting for, I never really understood. The point I'm trying to make is simple: do not let certain circumstances stop you. Keep moving forward. Forward motion is better than no motion. My first home was a notorious crack house throughout the mid '80s and most of the '90s. Before I bought it, I was only approved for a $120,000 home loan. I didn't want to buy that particular home but after a considerable amount of time and home searching, I realized that my eyes and thoughts were too big for my financial situation at that moment, and for that space and time in my life. That didn't mean that things would always be that way, so I kept at the search but modified my standards and expectations a little. If you change the way you view or think about a thing, then you will change the way you feel about it. So when that crack house was available I purchased it with no hesitation. That crack house helped pave the way for everything that I am doing now. Imagine if I would have been discouraged and had given up. I wouldn't be in the position I'm in at this moment. Don't allow certain circumstances to hinder you and eventually lead you to a space where quitting is the only option.

Once you own the property, you can do different things that a renter can't. For example, you can refinance for a better interest rate. Or better yet, refinance for a better interest rate *and* get cash out. Basically what I am trying to say is great things start from humble beginnings. If your approval doesn't meet your expectations, don't worry. Use it to buy a house, and use that house as a stepping stone for something better in the near future.

Selling a home is also a way to gain access to the

equity in it. There are pros and cons to selling your property but keep in mind that you have to do what best suits you, whether it's selling or refinancing with cash out. Both have benefits and drawbacks. An obvious benefit is the money gained from the sale. How title is held (whether it's a residence or an income property) will determine the taxes owed, or if any are owed at all. If the home was a personal residence and you lived there for two years or more, then there won't be any tax on the profit, up $250,000 if single. If you're married, $500,000 capital tax is exempt. The drawbacks, if the property was earning you an income, can be that the home is considered a business and is taxable. Not only that but you forfeit future earnings because of the sale.

One of the biggest contributing factors that an underwriter considers is something called debt to income ratio or DTI. DTI compares your debt to your income. Lenders use the debt to income ratio as a standard to check your ability to pay your monthly bills and the repayment of debt. DTI is calculated by dividing monthly debt by gross monthly income. For example, Tobias pays $1,200 each month for his mortgage, $500 for his debts and $300 for his car loan each month. His monthly debt adds up to $2,000. If Tobias' gross monthly income is $6,000, his DTI would be 33% ($2,000 ÷ $6,000 = 0.33). In this example, Tobias has a reasonable DTI percentage. 43% and under is what lenders like to see.

The lower the debt to income ratio, the better chance you have of securing a home loan. Of course, a high DTI is frowned upon because it informs the lender that there is too much debt compared to income. A lower DTI is obviously more desirable because borrowers are more likely to succeed in completing monthly payments.

***

Looking For the Right Property

Once the loan is approved, it's now time to look for a home. Location is the key with real estate. When searching, keep in mind that this will have long term effects on you financially. If you find a good location, move on it. Do not hesitate; if it's a good deal and works for you then pursue it. I suggest finding a good Realtor or broker to answer any questions you might have.

A lot of good deals are found in financially depressed areas. The hood often has great opportunities for a savvy investor. The key is knowing the area and it helps if you know people in that neighborhood. Something as simple as knowing the lay of the land can make a huge difference.

When I was a teenager, a guy purchased a home in my neighborhood that had been vacant for years. He had workers that were renovating the property. The problem was no one in the neighborhood knew him, so when the home was finally finished someone stole all the new upgrades. They went in and took everything; this guy had done a major renovation - new kitchen and bathroom, copper pipes for the plumbing - everything was stolen. It is wise to do your homework when buying in certain areas. There are all sorts of options that investor could have exercised; introducing himself to the neighbors, hiring security, or have a family member live on the premises until the property sold. If the area is unfamiliar to you, I recommend that you at least meet the neighbors; it could save you a lot of money down the road.

There are many different ways to obtain a property. It just depends on the person or people involved, and every situation is different. If you have trouble securing a loan, one way to purchase is a lease option, or lease to own. I personally have not purchased this way, but I have advised several people who have chosen this route.

A lease option may be more appealing to a first time home buyer if their credit isn't so good, or if money is an issue. Sometimes when purchasing a home there are large amounts of money being transferred. For example, a home costing $100,000 may require 20% as a down payment, or $20,000. Putting 20% down insures that you do not have to pay PMI (private mortgage insurance). Most people do not have large sums of cash laying around so a lease option could be a fairly reasonable alternative.

PMI is insurance for the lender in the event that the buyer defaults on the loan. The lender requires PMI when the buyer has less than a 20% down payment based on the asking price of the home. If this is the case, then the cost of the loan will be increased and your mortgage will increase as well because of the private mortgage insurance costs. PMI isn't a tax deduction but the interest on the loan is. A 20% down payment on the total price of the home has its benefits because it will guarantee a lower mortgage and means you also own more of the home (equity).

The requirements are basically the same as renting an apartment - first, last, security deposit and a credit check. Most likely there will be a term that will require that the home be paid off in full in a certain amount of time. That term could be five years or more or less, but whatever the time frame, funding should be secured. If funding is not secured, then the seller and buyer go their separate ways and the seller retains the property.

***

Purchasing

I purchased a property with two homes on the land. Usually properties of this type are duplexes or a home with a mother in law unit, but that wasn't the case with this property. Everything was separate; the addresses were different and there were separate gas, electric, and water lines for each home.

This was huge because I could rent both units and the tenants would be responsible for their own utilities. If the homes shared water, gas and electric lines then I, as the landlord, has to pay utilities. The reason is simple, there wouldn't be any real way to determine which home used which amount of each utility. Also, if for some reason a problem occurs, then it can be dealt with individually. Anything can and will happen as it relates to a home and the landlord is usually the one that has to solve those problems.

There are many ways to do things but as far as real estate goes I only know of three different ways to earn money from it. That doesn't mean that other routes don't exist, I simply only have experience in these three paths.

1) Buying with the intention to flip, meaning you are buying a property solely to sell it. I have never purchased with the intention to resell, but I always think in the back of my mind that if for whatever reason I want out, I could sell. Generally I'm in it for the long haul. I collect rent month after month and year after year. It's a good way to earn passive income if it was bought correctly. There are many different factors for buying a home to determine if there is enough value to purchase: location, condition of the entire property, and the asking price. There are many more factors to consider when purchasing a home but I am not a Realtor; these are just my experiences. I can't reiterate enough how important it

is to find a good Realtor or broker to answer any questions you might have.

2) Once you have the property rented to good steady tenants, then refinance. In order to refinance the property, there has to be equity. Let's say you bought a home for $200,000 then a year later it is appraised at $300,000. The difference of $100,000 is your equity. Refinancing is borrowing against the equity. You can borrow 65 to 70 percent of the equity; in this case $65,000 - $70,000. The mortgage will increase but not by much, depending on your credit score.

3) Use the money from the refinancing to buy another home then repeat the process.

Real estate values usually increase year to year. It is always a good idea to purchase property, no matter the market. The key thing is to buy right. It doesn't really matter if it's a buyer's or a seller's market, you can capitalize in any market. The thing is to know what you are doing. Fortunately, there are plenty of knowledgeable professionals that can assist you. Again, seek out help from a licensed professional, an honest Realtor or broker, and do not leave anything to chance. Read as much as possible about anything on the subject of real estate. There is nothing wrong with asking questions and/or seeking out help – it will save you from future issues. If you have a question or don't understand something, ask. This is one of the best ways to understand the process.

Whether you are purchasing for a flip (when you buy a property specifically to sell) or as an income property, fixers (a home that is not in move-in condition) can be the way to go. It really depends on you and what your needs are at the time. Typically a fixer will sell below market value which means that someone can typically purchase the home, fix it up, then put it back on the market for a profit.

These type of properties usually get swooped up quickly. Fixers are what investors look for and usually these buyers employ tactics such as all cash deals. A cash purchase is more enticing for a seller, simply because it will close (when the official transfer of property from seller to buyer occurs) quickly. If there aren't any encumbrances associated with the property, such as a lien (the legal claim of property in order to secure the payment of a debt. Depending on how long the lien has been in place on the property can determine the dollar amount owed), then all cash transactions usually close quickly.

I had been looking for a home to purchase for about a month when I ran across a three bedroom, one bath, single family home. It was definitely a fixer, but that was what I wanted. I wanted to create another stream of income, so my intentions were to rehab the property then rent it out.

I collected rent for one year, but keep in mind that I purchased the property with cash, meaning there wasn't a mortgage on the property yet. After a year, I started the process of creating a mortgage for this particular property. The reason was simple: the interest would be a tax deduction and I wanted to get back the money I spent at the time of purchase and on the rehab. And that was exactly what I did.

I cashed out almost $100,000 and, combined with the rent collected for 12 months, I made a small profit. The newly created mortgage was $765 per month, and I had close to $100,000 in cash. That was with an impound account (tax and insurance calculated into mortgage). In this type of arrangement, the property tax and insurance premium amounts are added to the mortgage, and you pay that entire amount each month. The money collected for the property tax and insurance goes into an account that is specifically just for those expenses, which is why it is called an impound account. When the insurance and property tax are due, the money is paid out to the insurance company and/or the county for taxes.

The asking price was $88,000 but the home was so far gone that it would cost a lot of money to rehab. I couldn't see myself paying that much for the property. At the time, there were properties on the market for $150,000 or more, but not much more. Real estate was on a downward spiral. People were losing their homes and walking away from them as well. Most homeowners were underwater - they owed more on the home than what the actual value was.

I had figured that it would cost around $50,000 to rehab the property. There was room for me to capitalize but I wanted to save as much money as possible up front. This property needed everything - electrical, plumbing, drywall, kitchen, bathroom, and floors and that was just the inside. $50,000 was a low number for a complete overhaul but I was confident that the work could be done for that amount or less, so I made an offer of $70,000 cash with the contingency (dependence on fulfillment of a condition) of closing in 15 days.

The seller agreed to the terms and I closed in ten days instead of fifteen, which was a good thing because if for some reason I didn't close in 15 days, I would have forfeited my good faith deposit of $5,000, which was applied toward the purchase price.

Once I received the keys, I went to work. The property was in bad shape but not to the point of no return. I hired a contractor to complete the task.

Some of the advantages to hiring a contractor to complete the work are:

1. The contractor will deal with the city as needed for permits, which are needed when taking on a

huge renovation project. This is just to ensure that certain things are done according to code. For example, electrical wiring has to be done a specific way in order to not cause a fire.

2. If anything was to go wrong because of negligence on the contractor's behalf, then I would have a course of action. Nine times out of ten, the contractor has a license and insurance. I do not recommend that you hire a contractor who doesn't have proper credentials.

My estimate of $50,000 to rehab the home was pretty much on point. With that number in mind I still searched for the best deal I could find. I knew that if I could save as much money as possible up front, then there would be more profit later on down the road. My intentions with this property were to create a passive income. I contacted a few contractors, got estimates, and hired the best contractor for the job. He did the total rehab for $35,000 - $15,000 cheaper than what I had originally figured. He took care of the inside and outside of the property, and also handled all of the permits that the city required. All I had to do was kick back and wait for completion.

Saving as much money as possible is key when purchasing or investing in real estate. Location is important as well, but buying right is paramount. Purchasing below market value is a great example of buying right. Upon closing, you automatically have equity in the property; buying at market value doesn't allow any room for equity. This doesn't mean that some time in the future there won't be equity, it's just a waiting game. Every property I purchased (except for one), I bought below market value. This makes a huge difference financially. The equity can be used to buy another property, start a business or anything that you desire. The bottom line is that buying right is good for creating wealth.

When the work was completed, I put the word out that I was looking for a tenant. It was relatively easy for me to find a tenant because of my career as a barber; I know many people through the shop. If you do not know many people, there are websites that can list the property for you. Also a simple 'for rent' sign in front of the property can attract potential tenants. Also, don't forget about social media; a picture and a brief post on IG, Twitter, or Facebook can go a long way in helping find the right tenants.

It took only a few weeks before I found a suitable family to move in. When renting to the public, you will need to do your due diligence such as background and credit checks. The last thing you want to do is rent or lease to a deadbeat tenant. They are often difficult to evict.

***

Escrow

Escrow is a deposit of funds, a deed, or other instrument by one person for the delivery to another person for completion of a certain event. It doesn't matter if you are the buyer, seller, lender or borrower, you want to be confident that nothing will change hands until every detail has been followed. The company holding escrow has the duty to safeguard the documents, deeds, or anything else while they are in the possession of the escrow officer, and to release those documents when appropriate. In the case of buying a house, the title of a property is held in escrow, and only when all stipulations of the escrow have been met will the title and any other related documents be released. The Realtor or broker will give the escrow officer the information for the preparation of your escrow, which includes instructions and documents. The escrow officer will process the escrow according to the escrow instructions. When all the requirements are met, then escrow will be closed. Each escrow is systematically different because there is more than one way to hold title. The escrow officer follows the same format, but situations are different based on a client's needs.

***

Closing Costs

Closing costs are fees that will be paid by either the buyer or seller and are due when escrow closes. There are typically a lot of fees associated with closing costs. The seller or the buyer pays at closing, but it can be negotiated. Maybe you don't want to pay the full amount of the closing costs; you can negotiate that the seller pay it or maybe pay half. Remember that he/she could say no, but it's always worth it to ask.

***

Residual Income

Residual income, or passive income as it is sometimes referred to, is money earned after an initial event. Some examples of residual income are as a landlord, where the tenant pays the property owner a monthly rent, and people such as songwriters, singers, and writers who receive royalties after they've release a song or book. Even inventors receive residual income from inventions and patents they've sold. The money will continue to come in the form of a check or cold hard cash. If done right, the residual income can continue for months or even years.

Just to be clear, I am talking about starting something that can last a lifetime. Usually this involves starting a business and through that business a lifelong income can be obtained. But it won't come easy. I know you probably heard the old saying, "If it comes too easy then it probably won't last." I am a firm believer of that phrase because every time something came my way and I didn't really have to work for it, it left just as easy as it came.

When you work for something, you respect it whatever it may be. In this case, I'm talking about money. If someone gave you some money to go shopping, nine times out of ten you are off to shop. But on the other hand, if you worked long hours throughout the week to earn that same amount of money, you would think twice about frivolous shopping sprees.

If you already have a job or a career, that is good. But in order to create true wealth you will have to start something that can generate a residual income. So what type of business can kick start residual income? One is to own or create anything that can earn revenue without you actually being there. If you are at the workplace it's by choice not force. That's the difference, millions of people work hard everyday and live paycheck to paycheck. With a residual income in place, your money is working for you.

If you are a landlord collecting rent month to month, you're getting a residual income. Keep in mind that as a landlord, certain things will be required of you besides just collecting rent, such as repairs. A tenant might call at 2am because a pipe broke and the basement is flooded. You as the landlord have to deal with it. I keep people in my circle that know how to fix certain things; for a busted pipe, I have three people that I can call. As a landlord you must have repairmen for every situation that may (and probably will) arise.

Another path to take as a landlord is to hire a management company. They screen all potential tenants, collect rents, and have access to repairmen when needed. But this comes at a cost. If you go that route, I recommend that you pick the best one that suits your needs.

CHAPTER 6

GRINDING T-SHIRTS

There is a lot of money to be made in the world of novelty t-shirts. In recent years people have been selling t-shirts as a way to earn a main, or even second income. It doesn't matter what the actual motivation is, the fact is that the t-shirt biz is big business. There are many different ways to capitalize. I can only speak to my own personal experiences, and they have earned me huge profits over the years.

To get started you need to know exactly what it is that you want to do. For example, there are many different types of shirts and a variety of methods that can be used to apply designs to the garment, such as heat transfer and silk screening. Let's say you have a design, maybe a picture with great detail and you want it on a t-shirt. Heat transfer is usually what most people use because it is quick; it doesn't take any time or major skill. The finished product looks good but it doesn't last long. After about three or four washes, the image sometimes begins to peel.

You might see a guy in a mall kiosk selling t-shirts with all types of different designs that can be applied to them. It doesn't take much space because the equipment is not huge, and large profits can be earned but the quality factor isn't there. I thought about using the heat transfer process in the past, but I wanted to build a brand. You can't build a brand with a product that is only good for a few machine washes. I needed something durable that would withstand time.

Silk screening was just the thing I was looking for; it's durable and lasts a long time. The shirt will actually fade before the ink in the design does. I have seen people wear a t-shirt I sold them ten years before and the logo was still on point, no peeling or fading. However, silk screening can be very expensive and there is a lot that goes in to it.

There are a bunch of fees for every step of the way. There is a fee for setting up, cleaning up, printing the image on the shirt, as well as costs for each color in the design. There is also a fee for each t-shirt. You also need graphic design, and maybe a graphic designer, which is expensive; however, if you can do graphic design yourself you'll save a lot of money. Once everything is paid for, you will have to sell the product at a certain price in order to earn a profit, or break even.

I tried to have a company print a design for me but there wasn't enough of a profit margin. I was told by the owner of the company that I couldn't expect to make a profit on the first run, and that I would start to see a profit on the second or third run. But I'm all about the profit so I began to look for a silk screen machine to print my own t-shirts.

Once I found a silk screen machine that was in good condition and at a reasonable price, I bought it. The guy I bought it from showed me how to use it, but it was going to take some practice if I was ever going to get the hang of it. I practiced and practiced but no matter what I did I couldn't get the image on to the garment correctly; it would always be slightly off center. After many failed attempts, I finally got the hang of it. The image wasn't perfect, but I was definitely getting better. I was printing my own product and it felt good.

The year was 1998 and I had an idea about selling t-shirts at the Bayou Classic in New Orleans. The Bayou Classic is an annual college football game between Grambling State University and Southern University. I ordered 2,000 t-shirts and didn't really know or understand how to use the machine. I just had an idea and ran with it. I didn't really put much thought into what would be involved with selling any product at the Bayou Classic, and not just any product but t-shirts, shirts that people will wear and keep for years to come. I just was focused on the money part.

There is nothing wrong with money or the want of it, but sometimes when you do things for the sole purpose of obtaining money, most likely it doesn't work out the way you intended. Sometimes a person can become nearsighted and see only dollar signs. This is what happened to me. I figured 2,000 t-shirts x $20 = $40,000. Simple mathematics, right? I shouldn't have a problem moving 2,000 t-shirts because ten times as many people were expected to be in attendance on the day of the game. I *knew* that I could sell 2,000 t-shirts at that event.

What I didn't take into consideration was the school colors. Each school has class colors and I totally ignored that key component. Rookie mistake. If I had simply paid attention to that one important detail, it would have turned out so much differently. The one thing I failed to do was think on all the levels of the business venture and journey I was about embark upon.

My brother, a close family friend, and I drove to Louisiana. I bought a Chevy Astro cargo van; we loaded the t-shirts and were on our way. T-shirts were stacked from the bottom to the top of this van. The drive was long and exhausting. We each took turns driving, stopping only for gas and food. It took us two and a half days to reach Louisiana.

The first day we set up our booth, I noticed that the majority of the people were wearing black and gold (Grambling's school colors) or blue and white (Southern's school colors). I totally didn't even think about the school colors and that one little detail turned out to be a huge mistake. School colors are a big deal and I didn't have either of the school colors incorporated in the designs I had for sale.

We didn't sell many t-shirts and as a result, we didn't even break even. The final count was $1,400 exactly, which was very disappointing on a few levels. I was distraught; $1,400 was unacceptable to me. The time and effort we put in to making the whole thing happen as well as the money invested had me frustrated. It took me at least three months of planning and it just seemed as if it was all for nothing. Everything I spent in total came to just over $10,000.

Needless to say the trip was a failure, but it wasn't a total loss. Even though I hadn't sold enough t-shirts to break even, the experience was well worth the expense. I learned the value of preparation, and that failure has a way of showing you how to succeed. You just have to be open to it. You have to be optimistic even when you fail so you can learn and grow, which is exactly what I did.

On that long drive back to California, I had time to think. I did a lot of brainstorming instead of complaining about how things turned out. Complaining would have put me and everyone around me in a negative state of mind. Negativity is contagious, just like positivity. A positive environment is always better to create from.

When I wasn't driving, I wrote down my ideas no matter how ridiculous they seemed. When dealing with ideas you never know which one could be the one that makes the most sense. Even if a particular idea at first seemed ridiculous, I wrote it down. All it takes is for one really good idea to help, stimulate, or motivate you into an action or actions that can and will change your life.

Writing all of my thoughts and ideas down had me physically and mentally exhausted. Once I was well rested, I read and re-read what I had written down on that long ride home. Nothing jumped out at me at first. I went back to work, back to the business of cutting hair. Then boom! Out of nowhere *Ridaz Wear for Ridaz Only* popped into my head. I was overwhelmed with happy positive thoughts.

Ridaz Wear sounded good to me. Motorcycle enthusiasts and people in general gravitated towards the brand. During that time, many young black males in the hood considered themselves or wanted to be a 'ridah'. Tupac has a song entitled "Ambitions of a Ridah", and a number of the youth of that era considered themselves ridah's. I knew that Ridaz Wear would appeal to them. I didn't want it to be considered a negative brand, so I came up with an acronym for it - Representing Intelligent Determined Americans with Zeal. I really wanted people to feel empowered while wearing my brand.

Many motorcyclists liked it because it symbol-ized riding out and enjoying the day. The demographic that I was targeting was males, ages 15 to 30, but anyone was welcome to purchase and wear the t-shirt. I dealt with a lot of high school kids because my shop was right down the block from a high school. I knew basically what the kids wanted to wear and the product reinforced what they were already wearing. The majority of the kids just wanted a nice clean t-shirt that matched their shoes.

That was the thing, matching colors. The t-shirt had to match the latest shoes that were out at the time. It seemed like everyone was wearing Jordan's brand of shoes, so I would make sure that I incorporated the shoe color into the t-shirt. I had a subscription to Eastbay catalog, and within the pages of that catalog were all the latest shoes - Nike, Adidas, Reebok, and every other shoe known to the athletic world; I matched t-shirt colors based on the latest colors of those popular shoes I had seen in that catalog.

Before you put together a design and start selling it, there is something that should be considered - proof of concept, which in short means that a product has to be proven to be an ideal seller before being sold in large quantities. How can the product be proven? One way is to do a test run. Whatever it is, in this case t-shirts, ask different people what they think about it. Post on social media sites and see what type of response you receive. If it is positive, do a printing and begin selling.

It was fairly easy for me because I printed my own t-shirts. I remember trying to learn how to use my silk screen machine. No one would help, it seemed as if people enjoyed not contributing to a person's success. At least that was my thought at that particular time, but in actuality there are many people who are willing to help an individual succeed in life or business, or just about anything that you want to do. You just simply need to know where to look.

Phunky Phat Graphics was the place to go if you needed any type of promotional material done - fliers, posters, album covers, billboards, t-shirts, you name it. If it related to graphics work and promotional materials, they were the authority. I had hired them on many occasions for the production of fliers, business cards, and t-shirts. I figured since we had a decent relationship, the owner wouldn't mind explaining and showing me the fundamentals of printing t-shirts. Boy, was I wrong. He wanted me to do an internship for six months, with no pay. I politely declined. I had my own business to run. I couldn't work my business and intern for free; my business would have suffered.

I went to work on learning how to use the silk screen machine and eventually got better and better. Soon I was printing all of my own designs and logos, which was a blessing because that saved a lot of money. I didn't have to pay someone else to print for me.

More and more people began to buy the shirts. I would be driving down the road and would see people that I didn't know wearing Ridaz Wear. That was a big ego booster. People were seeking the brand out. Word of mouth was a big contributor to sales. I was selling the t-shirts for $20 and hoodies for $30. Eventually a few mom and pop stores began to purchase the brand as well.

I had a special price for store owners and vendors. I couldn't expect to have the same price point for vendors as the public, especially if they were buying in bulk. This is where printing my own product came in handy. For vendors, t-shirts went for $8 each and hoodies for $20. Ridaz Wear did very well in the stores. You could buy it from the store as well as from me, but the stores gave the brand legitimacy. People that knew me and saw Ridaz Wear in stores would say, "You're in the stores now!", which helped create a buzz and improve business.

I would sell more t-shirts and hoodies when I hit the streets. Every Sunday and sometimes on Monday my friend Bob and I would ride around selling shirts. We would drive from the east to the west and to some of the neighboring cities. I would drive right up to wherever the dope spot was located. Why? Because that's where the money was. Drug dealers had cash in hand ready to spend.

Bob was a natural salesman; he could sell a shirt or hoodie to anyone. I've seen him approach people and they would be shaking their heads saying, "No thanks." But Bob wouldn't quit and eventually they would give in. Bob had the gift of gab.

I wouldn't recommend to anyone that they go to drug areas to sell products. There are more ways to move a product these days without the risk of being in the wrong place at the wrong time. The internet has opened up doors that can change anybody's life with the right idea or products. T-shirts are one of the most common things sold online, but it isn't easy. Just because you have a website and a great logo or design doesn't mean that it will translate into sales.

You need to make sure that the design or logo is something that the people are feeling, something that they can identify with. The process can be time consuming but it can be simple. This is a crucial step that should not be avoided. Some people can come up with ideas and concepts as easy as 1, 2, 3. Are you one of those people? I know that I am not, but I do have my moments and I'm sure that you do as well.

Proof of concept will let you know more than anything if you have a product worth backing financially. No one wants to put a lot of money behind a product that tanks, so proof of concept is you using a small amount to back the product and make sales. Not to your family or friends because they are probably biased.

Say you think you have a very good logo for your t-shirt clothing line. Instead of printing a large number of shirts that haven't been proven yet, you print one dozen. With t-shirts in hand you begin the process of selling to the public, a public that doesn't know you from a can of paint. If you can sell all of your product in a reasonable time frame (reasonable for one dozen in my opinion shouldn't be no more than two days), you've got a potentially successful product.

Printing the t-shirts myself allowed me the ability to experiment with different designs and slogans. Not all went well but that was okay because I cut out the middle man and was doing the work myself, which saved time and money. I didn't have to wait on anyone or any company; I would have an idea and immediately went to work on making it a reality in the form of a design on a shirt. I saved money because no middle man was looking for a pay day.

I tried a variety of different slogans. One that stood out and sold fast was, "Real Ridaz Wear Ridaz Wear". The shirt itself was all black and the letters were silver so the t-shirt also appealed to Oakland Raiders fans. Once you establish the logo or name that you wish to brand, it is recommended that a trademark search be done. This will let you know if someone is currently operating a business using the same name. If everything is clear then proceed to trademark the name. A trademark protects you as the owner of that name - any name, symbol, figure, letter, word, or mark adopted and used by a manufacturer or merchant in order to designate his or her goods and to distinguish them from those manufactured or sold by others. A trademark is a proprietary term that is usually registered with the Patent and Trademark Office to assure it's exclusive use by its' owner. Once you have trademarked the name, you are legally protected as the owner from theft and knock-offs. Now it's time to start production on any scale that you choose, large or small.

There are many options for an entrepreneur to take advantage of. For example, you can do as I have and print the garments yourself. Although printing yourself will save you money in the long run, it is time consuming. If you don't know how to operate the different machines and tools needed then time will be spent learning. Another alternative is to outsource. Both have advantages; it just comes down to your needs. Obviously the advantage of outsourcing is saving time, time that can be utilized in different areas of your life. The advantage of doing it yourself is saving money.

There is another way to become a t-shirt entrepreneur. Teespring is a platform where you can have t-shirts made but no money is exchanged until someone buys your shirt. You have to make the design yourself or hire a graphic designer to design it for you. Once the design is complete, it's submitted to the Teespring staff by way of their website, www.teespring.com, who then create the shirt on demand, meaning that they print them out only when someone buys one online. Then it's time for you to market and advertise. Most people advertise on Facebook; they offer paid advertising. For more information about Facebook ads, login and find the best plan for you.

***

Ambition and Hustle

Ambition and Hustle is something that I would mention from time to time when motivating my clients. Not all of my clients need motivation but then again you never know what someone is going through. When I feel someone can benefit from a good pep talk, I'm there to help. One day, the words "ambition and hustle" came flowing out of my mouth, and I thought, "Wow, that would make a great t-shirt design!" And so it began in the summer of 2012: Ambition and Hustle, or A+H for short.

Ambition and Hustle has many different meanings but the foundation of its meaning is a basic step by step formula. It's simple math – *ambition + hustle =*

money, a home, a car, and women.

Ambition is desire, your desires, the thing or things that you want in life. But no matter how much you desire or want something, without action the thing desired will never be achieved. It'll just live in those thoughts as something you want but never comes to fruition. I've run across many men and women who have never reached their full potential and have accepted it as just the way things are but that isn't necessarily true; you can do anything that you put your mind to.

Hustle is the part of the equation that turns ambition or your desires into reality, it is a key component. Hustle is the action that can make everything fall into place, no matter what it is. The word hustle throughout the years has been associated with street level crime. That's not the case at all as it relates to Ambition and Hustle. It's all about improving your situation in life.

The money is the fruits of your labor, the sum of your ambition and hustle. Whether you work for a company or are self employed, money will be earned and whatever is done with it will determine your quality of life. Money isn't everything but try living life without it. We can't live without oxygen or water and money is the same way. A life without money can be very difficult. I don't know about you but life is short and I want to live it on my own terms.

The house represents what should be purchased with the money earned. We live in America, the richest country on planet Earth, so if you own a piece of America then you own a piece of the richest country.

The car represents what could be bought by using your home, or another home could be purchased to keep building a passive income. If a car is bought the right way, a lot of money can be saved. For example, if you own a home and there is enough equity in it then you can borrow against it. Once everything is finalized, take that money and use it to buy a car outright. If you buy from a car lot and use their financing, the interest rate can be high and you will have a monthly car payment. By using your home's equity, you can cash out more than what is needed.

I will use $100,000 as the benchmark for this example. Say you refinance with a $100,000 cash out. Depending on your credit, the mortgage might increase by three to four hundred dollars. You now have $100k to do with however you choose.

So now you buy that car that you've always wanted. Let's say it costs $50,000 with license and taxes, which will leave you with $50,000 to invest in perhaps an income property. The interest paid on the loan is tax deductible; regular car financing isn't. It only makes sense to own property in America. I can't say this enough: home ownership is one of many different ways to build wealth.

The last component of the Ambition and Hustle equation is the woman (or a man for the ladies). Generally, people are more attractive to the opposite sex when they appear to be secure on all levels, not just financially. But Ambition and Hustle is a brand that hopes to instill financial awareness and growth, so once the equation Ambition + Hustle = Money, a Home, and a Car is solved, the women (or men) will come. Don't chase the honey first. Chase the money; the honey's come with the money.

I have enjoyed some success from Ambition and Hustle but on a minimal level. RidazWear did huge numbers and that's what I really wanted back when it was launched. With Ambition and Hustle, it was more about instilling a state of mind to make people aware of financial situations. Trust me, there are different routes to get to the money, but for me this equation is pure and simple, tried and true.

As the brand is all about financial awareness, I wanted the person wearing my product to feel good every time they wore it. Not solely because he or she looked good in the product, but because they recognized the truth in the equation and was inspired by it and through that inspiration, they would hopefully put the equation into action.

Ambition and Hustle is real; it has the power to change a life. My life has been transformed not only by this equation but also by the different principles throughout the pages of this book. Bottom line - it comes down to you. In order for change to occur you have to be willing to sacrifice time and, in some instances, money. I have a rule that I've been living by for some years: sacrifice today for a better tomorrow.

I missed out on many so-called 'epic nights' out on the town. While many of my family and friends were out having fun living it up, I was at home reading or studying different online courses trying to advance myself. I understood that by advancing myself, I was advancing my family. Sacrificing today means not doing certain things that will keep you broke tomorrow. If you are living paycheck to paycheck, then you don't need to be doing anything but figuring out how to save money, not going out and spending it. That money spent could be put into a savings account to help fund the future that you want and deserve.

It's not easy and will require discipline as well as vision. The ability to see the light at the end of the tunnel that you are traveling through will serve you greatly. I found pleasure in knowing that all the things that I was doing was going to pay off soon. That's how having vision can benefit you - you have to be able to visualize yourself in the position that is to come as an result of your past sacrifices. This will help motivate you whenever you find yourself in doubt. I found comfort in knowing that my sacrifices were going to pay off one day soon.

Trust that the day *will* come soon enough but until then have peace in understanding that your labor will not go unrewarded. Stay focused and optimistic and may all of your dreams become reality.

CHAPTER 7

ROADS TO SUCCESS

There are many different roads that can lead to one's personal success. However, without personal discipline nothing can be accomplished. You will need to stop all the things that are counterproductive to your financial future in order to live a life on a higher plane.

The ability to go and do as you please is priceless. To be able to vacation whenever and wherever is something that most people can only dream of. Money has the power to enhance life. It also has the power to ruin a life as well. Too much of anything can be detrimental to anyone. There is a lesson to be learned when dealing with the struggles of life. Either you learn or you are doomed to repeat the same mistakes, like a CD player on repeat. That is how the majority of us are - we repeat the same financial mistakes over and over again.

The following are examples of two people who came from a low economic background but still were able to rise above their circumstances. Just because you are born into a bad or tough situation doesn't mean that it has to stay that way; there are things that can be done to alter your current reality. These two gentlemen have changed and altered their lives and futures for the best, they simply believed in themselves and pushed beyond what was and is considered to be 'normal' in their environment. Both men, through real estate, found security, wealth, and peace of mind.

***

MIKE

Life can be a very complicated journey but like with most things, you get back what you put out. This is true. You can't honestly expect to make lemonade with oranges. If a person wants to do something special and productive with their life then all that is needed is to simply apply yourself in a special and productive manner. Good things can only come from good, and bad can only come from bad. Whatever path you choose, whether it's on purpose or by way of bad decisions, you got there on your own accord. That doesn't mean that all is lost if you travel down the wrong path. As long as you are living and willing to make a change it can and will happen. That is the case with Mike.

Drugs and alcohol are vices that many people in the United States battle daily. Mike fought his addictions to drugs and alcohol for years until finally he had enough and decided to make something positive happen in his life. That is when changes happen for the best, but you must be willing and open to those changes. Nothing happened until he made up his mind. That's where it all starts, in the mind. The body will follow whatever instructions the mind gives, so learn to control your thoughts and in time, you will control your destiny.

Mike's transformation is amazing considering that many people do not make it out of the trap of drug and alcohol addiction. He gives all praise to God, for without Him none of us would exist. Mike has owned 24 properties simultaneously - great income! However, it's only a great income if you buy right. That is what Mike stresses the most, "Buy right!"

I asked Mike how an individual 'buys right' and he responded, "It's okay to have debt ratio if you can afford to keep it. The only way you can afford to keep it is if there is enough equity in the property and you purchase below market value. That's how you buy right." Debt ratio, as explained previously refers to the debt to income ratio, or DTI.

He suggests riding around the area that you live. Find a home that looks as if it's a burden to the owner and try to make contact. Some homeowners have income property for which they are landlords but over the years it has become a burden. How does a property become a burden? There are actually many different reasons but it really boils down to the owner and what he deems a burden. Tenants that are always late with paying the rent, constant calls for repairs, or just unruly people who may cause bad situations for the neighbors. Maybe the owner fell behind on taxes and can't afford to pay them. Mike says in his experience tenants parking cars on the grass is a big problem because that can kill the grass and is unsightly.

Whatever the situation, once you find a potential property then it's time to make contact with the owner. Mike recommends that you go to the county records where all deeds of trust are recorded as public information, and get the owner's address. Once you have the address you can:

•Write a letter expressing your interest in buying the property and/or

•Go to owner's home address. "Go to the owner's

home and talk with him/her about selling," Mike says. In his experience, mailing a letter doesn't get the job done. Personally, I think it would be good to mail a letter *and* to pay the owner a visit. You might hear many no's before you strike gold. That one 'yes' will be worth all the "no thank yous" that you may encounter.

Another route that is beneficial for an investor is to buy first phase homes. First phase homes are homes that are new that have recently been built. They might have ten phases who knows, but Mike suggests that you buy at the first phase level. The logic is that if you purchased during the first phase you will have gained equity by the time the developer finishes all phases, which can sometimes mean a lot of equity. That is *your* money that can be tapped into whether you refinance or sell. Google "home developers" and you will find a list of developers and locations of ground breaking sites to choose from.

First phase or new home developments are homes that are built by a home development company. A real estate developer will buy acres of land with the intention of building and selling to the public for profit. Within the first phase, as Mike likes to call it, there are opportunities that most people overlook, but not Mike. Mike says, "You can buy a new home with the intent to sell at a later date."

Mike bought six homes all in the same area with the same real estate home developer. When the homes were finally finished, he found tenants for each one. Finding tenants is a process that can be tedious but is vital because a good tenant is invaluable, so use diligence when screening for potential tenants. Section 8 is what Mike recommends, because Section 8 pays the majority of the tenant's rent. Section 8 is a housing voucher program funded by the U.S. Department of Housing and Urban Development.

After two years Mike sold all six properties. He earned $100,000 or more from the sale of *each* property, and also collected rent for close to two years. That is over $600,000 in profit; not bad for almost two years of ownership. I don't know many people that earn $600,000 in two years or less. How long would you have to work at whatever it is that you do before you earned $600,000?

***

CHARLES

The background for this individual is similar to that of many that grew up in an environment of lack. You learn quickly how to survive, and not just how to survive but how to thrive. As a kid, I walked down the street and passed all the drug addicts and dealers with their flashy cars and jewelry on my way to school. I remember thinking, "Damn, I want that!" Like so many kids in the ghettos throughout the U.S., I knew that something had to change. If I wanted the things I saw on a daily basis, I would have to hustle hard for it.

Charles grew up in the city of Oakland, California. The streets of Oakland was and still is a rough place to grow up. Charles sold dope (cocaine to be exact) and pimped women. For twelve years he hustled, dealt with the ups and downs that came with the game. I say game but please understand that it isn't a game; the prison sentences that get handed down to defendants are unreal.

Charles eventually went to prison for his transgressions for four years and five months. He knew that it couldn't last forever and wanted to get out of the game. Learning from his mistakes and advancing on to a better situation is a trait that he possesses. When he paroled, it would have been easy to go back to a life of crime. After all, selling dope and pimping was in him.

Instead, Charles choose to invest in real estate and that proved to be a wise decision.

Real estate is a good opportunity for anyone because it doesn't require you to have a degree. All that is required is a desire and will to find and make deals. Charles actually purchased a home for $20,000 that was worth $250,000. That seems almost impossible in today's market but deals like this do exist, you just need to know where to look. That is where you will need to tap into a deep desire and a will to fuel that desire. But how did he do it?

Charles had a lady friend whose mother owned a home that was free and clear (no mortgage owed) but the property had a $13,000 back tax lien. The mother lived in another state and couldn't keep the property maintained, and hiring a property management company didn't seem ideal. The property had become a burden to her and she just wanted to get paid something for it. If the tax lien went unpaid much longer, the property would be seized by the IRS.

The friend connected her mother and Charles, and the mother told Charles that all she wanted for the home was $20,000 but that it had a $13,000.00 tax lien. If he was interested in buying the property, then all that would be needed was the $20,000 and she would sign the deed over to him. However, Charles would have to pay the lien himself. After the transaction was finalized, Charles began renovating the property, putting about $10,000 into it. The total cost of the home, including renovation and the lien was $43,000 - not bad at all for a home that was appraised at $250,000.

There is money to be made in real estate, it just takes a little bit of patience and knowledge. I'm not saying that you have to go to school or take some type of real estate course, but a certain amount of understanding of real estate is required. Certain things cannot be rushed and real estate is one of those things, but when planned and executed properly the results will be life changing financially.

After Charles finished renovating the home, he rented it to a family for $1,500 a month. Remember, there wasn't a mortgage on the property so the rent collected was 100% his. He didn't have to pay a certain amount of money back to a bank or lending institution, because he paid for it with cash in full. Once the new tenants were settled in and were there for the long haul, he applied for and received a mortgage loan for $150,000. Charles earned a $107,000 profit from this transaction and was still in possession of the home.

Now Charles had a mortgage of $900 a month, and the rental income was $1,500 a month. He earned $600 in positive cash flow every month and he also had the $150,000 from the loan, a decent source of positive (or residual) income. Put your money to work for you so you can be free to do as you please.

Charles owns 17 properties that he collects a monthly positive income, an income that he doesn't have to work for. At the beginning of every month he has checks coming in from different tenants. Money in the bank! How would you like to earn money while doing whatever it is you really want to be doing? It can happen for you but you need to prepare yourself in order to reap the benefits.

Preparation is the key. How can you expect to benefit from anything if you have not put in the necessary work? Nothing in life is free; a free ride will more than likely arrive you at a destination that you do not like so always prepare yourself for the things that you want, otherwise you are forced to accept whatever comes your way.

Preparation comes in many different forms. School is a route that is frequently traveled. There are many types of schools that can be used to help advance your knowledge and skill set. Applied knowledge is simply using that knowledge. When using your knowledge, you are honing your skill set because you are gaining experience, and experience is the one thing that you can't forget because you've actually lived it.

CHAPTER 8

Q & A WITH SUCCESSFUL PEOPLE

JOSEPH CANNON

I had the pleasure of interviewing Joseph, a young man who has taken the profession of barbering to a whole new level. His story and the things that he has accomplished in a short period of time is truly inspirational.

Q - What is your name?

A - My name is Joseph Cannon.

Q - What is your occupation?

A - I am a barber, co owner of KJ's Barber and Hair Creationz and President of CanRoz Inc.

Q - Are you happy with your occupation, and is it ful-

filling?

A - Yes , I am happy with what I do for a living. It is fulfilling to be able to control my own schedule and do what I want without anyone telling me what to do.

Q - Yes, that is fulfilling for me as well. Nothing like working for yourself, what you put in is what you get back. How long have you been a barber?

A - I started cutting hair at the age of 15. I've been cutting professionally for 14 years, since 2002.

Q - I know that you own several barbershops and salons, how exactly did you get started? What made you want to cut hair and scale up to more than one shop?

A - What made me get started cutting hair was personally experiencing bad haircuts so I decided to cut my own hair. People would ask me who cut my hair and after telling them I did it myself, they wanted me to cut theirs. As time went on I got better and better. I was charging $5 and $10 at that time and my mom kept telling me I needed to go to barber college and get my license. After getting my degree in business management, I went to barber college. I always claimed to be a man of God, and one day my faith got put to the test. On the day I was going to take my barber license exam, my model for that exam faked on me. There was another guy with me that said, "Well, you always said you are a man of God, so step out on faith." and that's what I did. We went around asking random people if they would be my model and after being rejected numerous times, there was a homeless man standing on the corner asking for change. Long story short, he ended up being my model and I received my license. The reason I tell you this is because this is when my faith skyrocketed. After obtaining my license, I ended up in Fremont where I did *not* want to go, but my faith had grown so I decided to step out on faith. I was working there and Ken, the owner of the shop, had just bought the shop a couple of days before I started. Six months into the business, he changed the name of the shop to KJ's Barber and Hair Creationz. Six months after that, he had to sell the shop because his wife's job was relocating them. I was in a position to buy exactly a year from when I started there and all because I stepped out on faith. Now today there are six different locations: two in Tracy, one in Newark, Brentwood, Hayward, and San Leandro. The rest is history.

Q - What are the names of your shops?

A - KJ's Barber and Hair Creationz, KJ's Stylez, and KJ's Presents Divine Hair Designz.

Q - Did you attend college? I know that as a barber a person must meet state requirements through barber college or the apprenticeship program. But aside from that did you attend a business school?

A - I went to Menlo College where I graduated with my BS degree in Business Management in 2001. I graduated Moler Barber College in 2002. I opened first shop in 2003 in Fremont. I opened Hayward in 2007, the first Tracy shop in 2009, the second in 2013, then the first franchise in Brentwood in 2014, and the latest was in San Leandro in 2015.

Q - What exactly is your background? Where are you originally from?

A - I was born and raised in the city of Oakland, California. I was raised by both parents and saw the hard work both of them did by working and making things happen. I am a fair mix of both my parents. From my Dad I got strength to stand on my own and be firm with what I believe in, which helps me with running a business. My mom gave me the spiritual side of things and also a go-getter attitude. Today I am a devout man of

God as a minister preaching the gospel. I've been preaching now for nine years and God is truly blessing me. Growing up in the city of Oakland made it easy to get into trouble, but playing sports since I was nine years old kept me busy and taught me how to work in a team environment and work hard for what I wanted. I've worked a number of jobs since I was 15 years old: Blockbuster, FedEx, I was a security guard at Bay Fair Mall, I coached kids in Oakland, I did yard work and a lot more. It wasn't until I worked at 7Up that I decided I could not work for someone else anymore. That was in 2001 when I quit and haven't worked for anyone but myself since.

Q - What is the biggest obstacle that you have overcome?

A - The biggest obstacle I would say was raising my three kids with my wife while she wasn't working while being self employed and growing this business.

Q - What advice can you give to someone that wants to become a barber or own their own business?

A - To someone who wants to become a barber, I would say that's a great move, but in order for you to see that it is a great move you have to be consistent, like being at the shop when you say you will be there. Consistency is the main thing in barbering. Study your craft and always seek to get better; you can never know enough. Be humble and ask for help in areas that you feel you need. Be professional always and that goes with your presentation and your talk, and always remember customers are always right. To someone that wants to own their own business, all the above applies but to add to it you must understand that your vision is your vision and other people may not see or understand it. It's up to you to keep pursuing that vision so that one day they will see that vision, too. Don't be scared to take risks in helping individuals that no one else seems to want to help. People will try to tell you this or that won't work, but remember that they don't have your vision. I can recall numerous occasions when I was opening up another shop and people told me there wasn't enough people in that area that will get hair cuts. When opening early I was told people won't come early. With all that said I did not listen because I knew my vision and today I'm living that vision.

***

LESLIE SMITH

Leslie "Les" Smith is a close family friend. I have seen him grow from a child to an adult, and the strides that he has made in his life are nothing short of remarkable. He has grown in the real estate industry and is growing on a consistent basis, every day (Leslie.smith@outlook.com). A lot can be learned from this young man, so pay attention and enjoy.

Q - How long have you been in the real estate business?

A - I've been involved in the real estate business since 2005. I started off as a loan signing agent. A loan signing agent is a notary public who's certified in handling and explaining loan documents. In my loan signing agent business, I worked directly with real estate brokers and agents, mortgage brokers and title companies. I assisted with the final documents required to close on a purchase, refinances, and the sales of all real estate properties.

Q -You are a licensed real estate agent, correct? In this business hundreds of thousands of dollars and sometimes millions transfer from hand to hand, so to speak, so I know that when large sums of money are

involved sometimes greed rears its ugly head. Do you consider yourself to be an honest man?

A - Yes, I am a licensed real estate agent. But along with that, I am an active member of the National Association of Realtors, which makes me a Realtor. Being a member of this association requires that I uphold and follow a strict code of ethics. We must always do what's ethically right in regards to our clients and who we do business with. This code of ethics are in place because of the simple fact that as Realtors we have to be trusted with a lot of confidential information whether it be banking information for a individual buying their first home or delicate information for big corporations making large commercial real estate purchases. It's extremely important that each Realtor follow the code of ethics, and there are serious repercussions for not doing so. Outside of the Realtor title, I believe in being honest, straightforward, and show respect to any individual I deal with, business or personal.

Q - How long have you been a licensed real estate agent?

A - I became a licensed real estate agent in 2013.

Q - Do you like the business? If so why?

A - I love the real estate business. What makes the real estate business so interesting to me is the fact that the many different aspects present different opportunities for anyone looking to buy, sell or invest for short term and long term. The real estate industry is attached to everyone's lives, whether they're aware of it or not. The house you live in, the apartment building you may live in, the building you work in, the grocery store you visit for food, the school your kids attend; it's all real estate.

Q - Tell me some of the benefits of owning property.

A - The top three benefits of owning property in my

opinion are:

1. Tax Benefits: Being able to deduct the interested paid on your mortgage can offer a great break on your tax returns each year.

2. Appreciation: Real estate is an asset and it appreciates over time despite the recent housing crisis in 2008. As the population increases there will always be a demand for housing and commercial property.

3. Equity: Compared to paying rent, each mortgage payment helps you build available equity on top of the appreciation that builds on your property. This equity can be treated like a savings plan. If you build enough equity or your home appreciates and creates equity, you can tap into it with a home equity line of credit or cash out refinance, or you can sell to gain immediate access to that equity.

Q - Should a person buy and sell or purchase with intent to keep it?

A - I think a person should try to do both if they are able to. Buying and selling helps build short-term cash flow. For example, if you're purchasing a distressed property under market value (wholesale price) and renovate the property to sell at full market value (selling at retail), you create short-term cash flow. Buying with the intent to keep builds long-term wealth. An example of this would be buying property or properties and allowing your tenants to cover the mortgage on the property by paying you rent every month. Over the course of 15 years, your tenants will have paid your mortgage for you, helping you create equity along with the market appreciation that will have occurred with your properties.

Q - What are some of the advantages of investing in or owning real estate?

A - One of the best advantages of investing and owning real estate is the income that can be created from the properties you own by renting them to create cash flow. For example, you purchase a rental property and the mortgage on that property is $1,200 per month. Based on market rent, the property can be rented to a tenant for $1,800 per month, and you decide to do this. You've just created $600 per month in income. Now imagine owning five properties similar to your first rental that all average $600 per month in cash flow. You've just created $3,500 a month in additional income for yourself. Equity is another advantage that everyone who invests and owns real estate really enjoys. You can either refinance or sell your property to get access to the equity.

Q - How can someone who has never owned a home become a homeowner?

A - The very first step a first time home buyer must take in order to purchase their first home is to obtain financing. The best way for an individual to find out their options on obtaining a loan and purchasing would be to speak with a loan specialist at your local bank or a mortgage broker. I prefer a mortgage broker over the local bank because they can shop hundreds of different lenders to find the right loan suitable for a first time home buyer. There are grants and programs that also assist buyers with the down payment needed to purchase, even if the first time home buyer is tight on cash.

Q - Is it possible for someone without employment or credit to purchase property? If so, how can this be achieved exactly?

A - Credit and employment are the two key components to proving you can afford property. You will have to have one of the two to be able to purchase property. If you have employment and no credit, there are ways to build credit to show your worthiness of receiving a loan. A co-signer would be the first option in helping you purchase. Your co-signer's income will also assist as well. An individual with no employment but great credit would need someone with an income to assist with the purchase of the property. You can use the individual's income to receive a mortgage and request that you are on the title of the property.

Q - What motivates you?

A - My primary motivation is and will always be my family. My goal in life has been to always keep my parents and extended family proud of my progress in life and my accomplishments. I'll eventually start a family of my own so preparing for my future and becoming financially independent has also been my motivation.

***

T. BEN TAYLOR

The following is an interview with T. Ben Taylor, a real estate broker at Akwaba Real Estate and Funding, Inc., located at 4202 Dublin Blvd. #358 in Dublin, CA. (email - benrealmr@msn.com) I have used Ben to purchase a few homes in the past and I can say that he is a fair and honest man. Honesty can be a very difficult trait to find in the business of real estate, and when you find someone who possesses this important trait, keep that person in your circle.

Q - How long have you been in the real estate business?

A - I have been in the real estate business for 31 years. I got my sales license on April 15, 1985 and my broker's license on October 10, 1993.

Q - In this business, hundreds of thousands of dollars and sometimes millions transfer from hand to hand, so to speak, so I know that when large sums of money are involved sometimes greed rears its ugly head. Do you consider yourself to be an honest man?

A - Yes, as a licensed real estate professional, ethics and honesty are a state requirement.

Q - What inspired you to become a broker?

A - I always have had the ability to sell items. As a boy of 7 or 8 years old in McComb, Mississippi, I started selling flower seeds. As I became older, I knew I wanted to work for myself and real estate was the perfect avenue for me.

Q - Do you like the business? If so why?

A - Yes, I like the profession and also real estate is financially rewarding. I have the freedom of not working for someone else, which I truly adore.

Q - Tell me some of the benefits of owning property.

A – One of the major benefit is the income tax write off. Other benefits include financial security, bragging rights, and income producing property such as rentals.

Q - Should a person buy and sell or purchase with intent to keep?

A - Yes, one should sell (if at all) when the real estate market is high. Conversely, one should buy when the market is low, all things being equal.

Q - How can someone who has never owned a home become a home owner?

A - First, contact a licensed real estate professional such as myself and I will direct the process from that point.

Q - Is it possible for someone without employment or

credit to purchase property? If so, how can this be achieved exactly?

A – It's a very complex situation to purchase property without employment and/or credit. However, it can be accomplished on a case-by-case basis.

Q - What motivates you?

A - My Christ driven life, my self determination, and the joy of seeing someone get a property through my assistance.

***

DERRICK BEDFORD

Derrick has been through many ordeals but he has never let them stop him from achieving his goals. I have known him for years and have seen firsthand the transformation that has taken place in his life. He is a living testament of how powerful one's mind can be.

Q - What is the name of your brand?

A - iNeverWorry

Q - How did the name come about?

A - I started the company back in 1995 as Never Worry. Over the last couple of years the name changed because I have grown into a working professional, providing training and consulting. I wanted to do something different that represented who I am today. One day I was on Facebook and I saw a post that said iHustle, so I took the post and put Never Worry under it. A friend of mine saw the post and said, "Why don't you just put the 'i' in front of Never Worry?" I tried that and I liked the result. I did some research on the lower case 'i' and saw that Apple used it for information, intelligence,(i.e. iPad and iMac) and all of the good things that Apple stands for. Since that is who I am today - somebody who shares information and represents emotional intelligence - I thought that the lower case 'i' was a good fit for Never Worry, so it became iNeverWorry.

Q - You basically answered my next question, which is what is the meaning of Never Worry or as it is now called, iNeverWorry?

A - Just to dig a little deeper, the objective with the brand (and the subsequent rebranding since the mid '90s) is to have people feel as if they are emotionally intelligent when they wear the brand name. They put it on as a shield of armor against all the different emotions that they may experience throughout the day. What I truly believe is that if more people looked at life through the lens of emotional intelligence then we'll have an impact on culture - people making better decisions and having healthier relationships.

Q - I understand that you also wrote a book on the subject of emotional intelligence?

A – Yes. It was released last July on my birthday. The purpose was to illustrate the times in my life when I was emotionally intelligent and other times when I wasn't, and the impact of both.

Q - What is emotional intelligence?

A – Well, there are four components to emotional intelligence:

1 - Self awareness

2 - The ability to manage your reactions

3 - Social awareness

4 - Managing relationships

Throughout the book I use those different skill sets and

scenarios to help the reader be more emotionally intelligent in their work and personal lives.

Q - OK, so we talked about the book, which is a great read by the way. What other products do you offer? For example: hoodies, hats, sweat shirts, and have you found them to be profitable?

A – Actually, I only offer dry fit t-shirts, tanks for the ladies, and hoodies, but I'm getting away from the merchandising in terms of individual sales. In 2017, I will no longer sell my merchandise individually. The only way you will be able to obtain them is if you attend one of my seminars or if you purchase the book. I'm moving it to an 'exclusive' status because I don't want my business to be mistaken as a clothing line, similar to the Insanity Workout Program. You can only get an Insanity shirt if you did the workout, so when you wear the shirt, people ask, "You did the Insanity workout?" They look at you with admiration; it's like a badge of honor. That's the effect that I want to have with this brand. When people see you with an iNeverWorry product, they know that you either purchased the book or attended a seminar because it can't be bought separately. But to answer your question, my most profitable products are the seminars, trainings, and retreats. Bigger than the money part is that this is the most effective way to impact the people.

Q - How do you advertise?

A - Through social media platforms, my iNeverWorry Facebook page, my personal Facebook page (DB Bedford), or through my website www.iNeverWorry.com.

Q - What has been or is an issue or issues that you have overcome?

A - The ability to stay motivated, and having the courage to create goods or services without knowing how people will respond. When people are not responding, can you find the motivation to keep going? My biggest obstacle in my earlier days were when sales were not good. I don't necessarily subscribe to that today because I get it. Our reward in life is directly in proportion to the amount of service we put in. When you move the people, then you'll move the money.

Q - I know first hand that there is a lot of stress associated with business. Have you ever thought about quitting? If so, what made you not quit?

A - All the time, and more often than one would imagine. I think that is just humanity; sometimes you just want to let it go. You question yourself. Is it worth it? Are people listening? But what keeps me going is remembering why I started in the first place.

Q - Do you have any advice for anyone thinking of starting their own brand or maybe a way of thinking to help with their whole outlook?

A - Don't do anything that's not purposeful. Ask yourself what is your 'why'? Why am I doing this? Start there. Do not buy candy machines just to make an extra dollar, but if your goal is to have a healthier alternative, such as sugar free candy in the machines, that serves a purpose. It goes much further than buying just for financial gain, so do things for a purpose. Find a purpose and understand that money is made through goods and services. I would recommend services, because services are attached to a need. Goods are optional. But if you can get both goods and services you will win, so that is my advice.

***

NIKKI PAUL

Nikki Paul owns the clothing line, Mobbn Pretty. She has made major strides in her life as well as with her clothing line. Every day more and more women empower themselves while wearing Mobbn Pretty.

Q - What is the name of your brand?

A - Mobbn Pretty Apparel

Q - How did you come up with that name?

A - Originally my sister and I talked about possibly starting a t-shirt line focused solely on sayings, but after that initial conversation we never spoke about it again. So maybe two years later, I was in my car listening to Beyonce (Flawless remix featuring Nicki Minaj) and as I'm listening to the songs content I heard her say, "Paid sisters and mobbn pretty" and a light bulb just came on in my head. I said to myself, "That would be cute on a tee!" and the rest was history...inspiration can come from anywhere!

Q - What is the meaning of it?

A - Mobbn Pretty was designed for women who face day to day struggles and personal issues, all while doing it pretty. Women tend to have the weight of the world on their shoulders dealing with children, jobs, and businesses so I wanted to design comfortable, trendy tees that made women feel beautiful, confident and inspired.

Q - How long have you been in the shirt business?

A - I've been in business for 18 months now.

Q - As a brand, is there more that you offer besides t-shirts such as hats, hoodies, undergarments, and women accessories?

A - Right now I am solely focusing on tees. I have done a trial run with dresses, pencil skirts, crop tops, and hoodies, but I found it to be easier to just do fashion shows and offer pre-orders for the specialty pieces I show for the consumers to purchase.

Q - How do you advertise, or do you advertise?

A - I have advertised through Facebook, Instagram, boutiques, fashion shows, flyers, cards, etc. but the best by far is word of mouth and people being a walking billboard just by wearing my tees!

Q - Since you started, what have been some issues that you had to overcome as it relates to the business?

A - In this business, finding good solid people to work with is difficult. Either the prices were through the roof making it hard for me to make a profit, or the prices were reasonable but the work wasn't efficient and they couldn't fulfill an order in a timely manner.

Q - I know firsthand the stress that comes with starting a business. Have you ever felt like quitting?

A - It's funny that you asked that because I was thinking of letting Mobbn Pretty go for a while. But then I thought about all the people who love my brand and purchase my tees every single time they are released, and I told myself to keep pushing, I can't quit now. People are actually engaged in my brand, so I had to keep pushing and I still am.

Q - As a woman, is it difficult at times to make things happen?

A – No, I don't think it's hard at all for women. I actually think we have it a little bit easier. We are approachable, business minded, and nurturers. When we want something, we go get it and we are not seen as a threat.

Q - Most business start ups usually fail or take a few years before they turn a profit. Has business been profitable?

A - It's been 18 months and my tees sell out every time. I make a 75% profit by spending $5.00 to $6.00 (including the tee) to produce the shirt and I in turn sell them for

$20. I don't have much overhead except for the graphic designer, which isn't very expensive.

Q - Is the product in any stores? If so, how did you accomplish that? Was the process difficult? Explain the process.

A – Yes, Mobbn Pretty is in a few local boutiques. When I first started Mobbn Pretty I already had personal relationships with other business owners (mainly boutiques) who I had met by patronizing their businesses. I just presented my tee and told them about my new business venture and asked if they would carry my shirts for a small percentage off each shirt, and the rest was history.

Q - Do you have any advice for anyone that might be thinking about starting their own brand?

A - My advice would be to first think of a catchy name for your business. Do lots of research on branding, advertising, silkscreen companies, demographics, graphic artists, and mock focus groups. Be consistent, stay humble, be able to take constructive criticism, have a great professional attitude, always be kind, and be sure to lock everything down with a contract. Keep receipts and make sure you have your legal things in order like your seller's permit, business licenses, tax documents, etc.

***

RICK

I first met Rick at my barbershop, and later found out that he is a talented fashion designer with a lot to offer to the industry. He designs and customizes articles of clothing to give it a distinct look and feel unlike any other brand in the fashion industry. His website is www.leerickie.com and can be reached via email at rocriodesigns@gmail.com.

Q - What exactly is it that you do?

A - I am a fashion designer. I run and manage a company called RocRio Designs which produces seasonal capsule collections that are sold online and wholesale to stores.

Q - How long have you been in this particular industry?

A - I have worked in fashion for over seven years. I launched my online boutique and began selling to stores last year.

Q - Did you receive any training or pursue a certain level of education for this career path?

A - I attended San Joaquin Delta College where I studied fashion merchandising, as well as a summer course at San Francisco Art Institute where I studied garment construction.

Q - How long did you have to attend school?

A - 2 ½ yrs

Q - Can anyone learn this without a formal education in this field? If so, what would be required?

A - I don't think just anyone can be a fashion designer. I believe it's a skill that you are born with. However, I do think anyone can run a successful clothing company without formal education. The first step would be finding the aesthetic of clothing that you would like to market and produce. After that, produce a small collection and have some type of showing to let the market see what you're doing as well as gain brand recognition. This could take a couple of years.

Q - Do you have a brand? If so, what is the name of your brand?

A - Yes, the brand is called RocRio Designs.

Q - Are you finding success with RocRio Designs?

A - Yes, my brand is one of the best investments I've ever made.

Q - I understand that you make all of your own clothing products 'cut and sew', correct? What are some of the advantages to actually making clothing as opposed to buying blanks and printing on those?

A - Yes, I have a staff of two that cut and sew all of my designs after I design and make the sample. Producing designs and printing and having a t-shirt company are two different things. The advantages of creating my own designs is that I am not limited to a t-shirt, and the revenue is much greater

Q - What is a disadvantage with cut and sew, if any?

A - I don't see any disadvantages.

Q - Are any RocRio Designs in stores? If so, what stores?

A - RocRio is carried in OwlNwood Boutique, Taylor Jay Boutique, Show and Tell Boutique in Oakland, and PURE Boutique.

Q - What is the process of ushering a clothing product into a store?

A - Developing a line sheet is the first step. A line sheet is all the designs that you are producing at wholesale listed on paper. Included is the price of each garment at the wholesale rate, the minimum the buyer has to purchase to receive the wholesale rate, and the colors and sizes that the garments come in (online templates can help you create a line sheet). After that, research the stores that fit your design aesthetic and set up a meeting to pitch your collection to the potential buyer.

Q - How do you determine price points?

A - Prices are determined by cost of fabric, production, and labor. Once this is determined, you can see exactly how much it costs to produce the garment and decide what your profit will be. This will vary depending on the demographic you are marketing to.

Q - What has been the biggest struggle to date?

A - The only struggles I have encountered are finding someone to assist me with the business aspects of my brand. Being the designer *and* running the company takes a lot of my time. I work Monday through Sunday, constantly promoting and marketing my brand, shipping orders, responding to emails, reaching out to stores, as well as constantly developing new merchandise.

Q - Any advice to anyone interested in this career?

A - My advice would be to get a mentor that has a successful business in fashion and learn the ins and outs of the company. This will save you from making costly mistakes early on in your career as a fashion designer.

TESTIMONIALS

It is refreshing and inspiring to find people that unselfishly encourage others by sharing the wisdom they have attained through their own unique personal story. His words of advice are supported by his visible success and accomplishments that elevate him to be a role model to many of his friends and clients. In my own life, Dre has been an example of how focused determination can motivate you to overcome any adversity that may prevent you from reaching your goals. Dre continues to be one of the most consistent people I have met and continues to be the embodiment of an entrepreneur. His ambition has encouraged me to make successful strides within my own career. I appreciate every honest conversation I have with Dre because at the conclusion, I know I have just spoken with a person that sincerely wants me to succeed in life and as a person. During a haircut, I was given an analogy that compared the journey of reaching a goal to walking up a flight of stairs which has been very important in my life. Often we set goals for ourselves and soon see all the obstacles on that path. However, if we approached the process of reaching a goal the same as taking one step at a time to get to the top floor, then the goal seems much more attainable. *Phil*

***

I remember talking to Dre about trying to increase my credit so I could purchase a home, and he told me a few things I could do to achieve this. I honestly didn't think it would work but I figured it was worth a shot. I wanted to be able to check my credit score to determine whether or not his suggestions made a difference so I downloaded the Experian app. I checked the app almost every day to see if my score had increased, but it was always the same. After about two weeks, I got tired of checking and thought it was a waste of time. About a month after taking Dre's advice, I got an alert from the Experian app. I clicked the notification and immediately noticed my credit score had increased 19 points. I was juiced! A month later my score increased another 17 points. After the fourth month my credit score had increased by 65 points. My score went from a 575 to a 640 in only four months and now I am eligible to qualify for a home loan. The advice that I have gotten from Dre on repairing my credit has worked and has helped me tremendously. I really didn't know where to start. My score jumped up almost a hundred points in a few short months. *D. Powell*

***

I went into Creative Reflections one day to get a haircut and noticed Dre the owner sitting in the chair reading a book about credit repair. Up to that point we had not had any conversations about credit repair, it was just shop talk, but I had been doing my own research on credit repair and real estate because it was an interest of mine. The book he was reading then became a talking point. Dre told me that one of his goals was to have an 800+ FICO score, and that he was saving money to buy his first fixer upper to rent out to create a passive income.

Some time had passed and Dre had not only purchased his fixer upper but was now working on renovating it to be released to a tenant. When the house was ready, he was able to collect $1,600 a month from a qualified tenant. Ever since meeting Dre, our conversations have grown from just regular shop talk to meaningful talks about life, family, and ways to build wealth; our relationship has grown from his being my barber to being my mentor and adviser. *KB*

***

I have been a client of Andre's (a.k.a. Dre) barbershop Creative Reflections for over ten years. Dre is not only an amazing barber, he is also a good friend and a trailblazer. During the time I have known Dre, I have witnessed him overcome challenges and have watched him excel in many businesses: clothing, film making, real estate, and cosmetology. While patronizing his barbershop, I have had the opportunity to bounce business ideas off of him and he has shared vital insights. Andre has inspired me to dive into real estate; recently, I completed a real estate course and I am currently purchasing an investment property. During this process, Dre shared with me some of the ups and downs of being a landlord and investing in Oakland, a city where we both were born and raised. In my opinion, besides getting a great haircut, many people can benefit from talking to Andre about investing in themselves and having the courage to step out on faith. Dre is a role model every day and shows by example that you can do whatever you put your mind to, and to not allow where you are from dictate where you go in life. For that, I am inspired. *Jamar Mears, M.A. Counselor/ Instructor/ Program Coordinator*

***

Andre is my brother, and I feel that this book should have been written by him a long time ago. As long as I can remember, Andre has possessed the will and desire to not only earn money but to also flip it. His skills and abilities in general to get things accomplished lies in various areas, but earning, increasing, and sustaining wealth is a true gift. *William*

***

Every time I get a haircut, I learn something new from Andre. When leaving the shop I not only have a fresh haircut, I feel inspired as well. *B.*